God! Are You Even Real?

What Is Prayer, Anyway, When You Feel Abandoned By God?

By Q. Eli

While every precaution has been taken in the preparation of this book, the publisher assumes no responsibility for errors or omissions, or for damages resulting from the use of the information contained herein.

GOD! ARE YOU EVEN REAL? WHAT IS PRAYER, ANYWAY, WHEN YOU FEEL ABANDONED BY GOD?

First edition. May 10, 2024.

Copyright © 2024 Q. ELI.

ISBN: 979-8224590322

Written by Q. ELI.

Table of Contents

I dedicate this book to my wonderful husband, who has stood by my side in sickness and health and has loved and supported me, as well as my three exceptional children whom I love so dearly, my great friends who always have my back, and my sister, who has been there for me through it all. I thank God for the fantastic support he has blessed me with. I am very grateful for them all!

Introduction

We often hear the word *pray* when there is some type of crisis—when a war has broken out or a natural disaster hits. We also hear the word *prayer* when someone has lost a loved one. They are often told, "I am sorry for your loss. I will be praying for you." But, *prayer*—what is it? Why do it? Is God even real? If so, does He answer our prayers?

Prayer has always been a significant priority in my life. I can remember praying to God as a child about many things. I would just talk to Him as if I were talking to another person. In my young adult years, I began to pray the Model Prayer. Jesus taught this prayer to His disciples in Matthew 6:9-13 and Luke 11:1-4.

Although I prayed to God, I had no idea who He was, what a relationship with Him was, or how to pray correctly. I had not accepted the Lord into my life. I did not grow up in a Christian home. We went to church occasionally, and I remember getting baptized as a child. I even remember my dad bowing his head to pray over our meals, but there was no example of a genuine relationship, just religion. I never prayed and asked Him into my life. I didn't pray in Jesus' name. I was ignorant of all of these things. I was clueless about the Bible, the importance of reading it, and most of all, the need to live it out.

God wanted me to know Him and have eternal life in heaven, and have victory and intimacy with Him. There is no way we can have a deep relationship with a stranger. We can converse with a stranger but not profoundly or intimately.

It was not until my early twenties I discovered this truth when I encountered God in a co-worker's church I visited. No natural person prompted me, but there was a nudging in my heart to walk up to the altar. I knew my life was a wreck, and I wanted to be changed, healed, and freed from the chains of my sin and brokenness. I wanted God to work on me, in me, and through me. This decision is what sparked a desire for prayer in my life. I saw how my church's older women prayed enthusiastically and passionately about issues and people. They prayed like they knew God would answer them. They prayed with assurance. I, too, wanted that, so I asked God for that type of passion, ardor, and assurance, and He answered my prayer.

Today, I pray about everything from help with my household chores to my children, my marriage, the church, the homeless, human trafficking, and many other things. I bring it to the Lord in prayer, and I love that I can do this. God has broken the barrier of my sins between me and Him through salvation in Jesus; I can go to God about anything, and I know He hears me.

Prayer is not telling God what you want all the time but praying that His will be done, voicing your concerns, and being transparent about your feelings—yes, even the ugly stuff. God is never intimidated by our feelings and thoughts. What a beautiful thing! As for the timing of prayer, we must sometimes wait several months or years to witness those answered prayers, but I want to encourage you to keep standing on the Word of God and His promises.

Indeed, waiting on the timing of God is pretty tough! It can make you feel as if He is not concerned about what you are bringing to him. You may even question His existence, and it's okay. I have found myself questioning God's existence. He understands our humanity and knows our hearts. It's all about God developing our patience and character, though. Believing this truth can be challenging and frustrating. You can feel hopeless at times, waiting on the timing of God.

You will undoubtedly feel discouraged sometimes if you are in a challenging situation and still waiting, but I hope you continue praying and believing. Trust Him—His yes, His no, His not right now, and those moments when He is silent. God's plans and timing are perfect even when we don't understand them.

I have taught and encouraged many individuals to pray and continue to pray with and for many. Prayer is a huge part of my life, and I humbly recognize I always need it and others do as well. So, my prayer for you is that as you go through this book while journaling, you will experience intimacy with God and be enlightened and strengthened in your prayer life and relationship with the Lord.

Chapter 1
What Is Prayer, Anyway?

"Answer me when I call to you, O God who declares me innocent. Free me from my troubles, have mercy on me, and hear my prayer" (Psalm 4:1).

So, what is prayer? Prayer is communicating with God through praise, thanksgiving, and intercession. To pray is to address God with adoration, confession, and supplication. Prayer is a conversation with God. Prayer is dialogue, not just monologue. Try taking some time to sit quietly and listen after you communicate with God. God speaks in silence. When we are silent, God is speaking. When we quiet our minds, God speaks. If we are overwhelmed with worry, our minds are not at peace, which may cause us to miss what God is trying to say. As you do this, expect to hear God speaking. Write down in your journal what comes to your mind. If you do not get anything right away, do not be discouraged. Sometimes, God speaks to us when going about our typical day. It could be that small voice in your head, a person, a billboard, a book, and, of course, the Bible. Sometimes, you may wait and wait to hear from Him.

Truthfully, it will feel like God is ignoring you at times, but know this is untrue. I feel like this now, like God has left me hanging, like He has abandoned me, forsaken me. I feel like I am not a priority for Him. The waiting and the silence make me feel like He doesn't care about me, so why should I keep going to a God who has deserted me? But with all these feelings of rejection, I know I have to keep pressing into His presence by faith when there is no sense of Him and I feel like I have nothing left in me to give! My fight has turned into exhaustion. My waiting has turned into frustration.

In all of this, though, I have made a conscious decision to believe He will answer, direct, and allow me to see what all the waiting is about. I am not saying that making a conscious decision is easy, but I know I must do this to gain victory over this spirit of defeat I am experiencing. I am hanging on by the thread or hem of the Savior's garment and looking for His voice in the silence. I know God can communicate through different avenues, but His answer will always align with His character and Word and confirm what we already know, so SPEAK, Lord!!! PLEASE!!

God has communicated with man since the beginning. We know Adam and Eve were the first humans to communicate with God (Genesis 3:8-19). God created both male and female for His glory, to rule over what He created, and to be in a relationship with Him (Isaiah 43:7). Everything we do should bring glory to God (1 Corinthians 10:31). Waiting on His timing also brings God glory. God, our Creator, takes pleasure in us (Psalm 149:4). He desires to fellowship with us daily through communication, even when we are not seeking fellowship with Him.

On the contrary, the enemy, Satan, loves it when we are not spending time with God. He knows the more time we spend with God in prayer, the more we become aware of His voice, His character, who we are in Him, and how He sees us. When we pray, we also grow closer to God and allow Him to work in us, through us, and for us. God patiently awaits us to come into His presence and commune with Him. Don't let the enemy persuade you otherwise.

God communicated with His people throughout the scriptures and still talks with us today (Hebrews 1:1-2). We must continue communicating openly with God daily and know He always listens to us. Knowing God intimately will determine how much time we spend with Him, our perspective of Him, and what we receive from Him.

I have known God as my Lord, as my Savior, and as the Sovereign One, meaning He tells me what He wants and has saved me from eternal damnation, from hell. He has the final authority in everything. I have heard people refer to God as their Friend and Good Father, but I don't know what it is like to view Him that way. I have come to realize I am struggling with this because my earthly father was great when he wasn't drinking. When he was drunk, he became violent and angry. He was physically abusive to my mother and to me, as well as to my younger siblings. My father had anger issues.

As stated before, when my father was not drunk, he was a fantastic dad. My dad was very affectionate. He always hugged me and my siblings and told us he loved us. He taught me to be considerate of others, express my feelings by talking to him, and many other great qualities. Yet he expected me to be responsible for my younger siblings at an early age. If I didn't look after them as he expected me to, I got a beating in the worst way.

This paradoxical relationship with my father caused me to view God as a Father in that light. I thought God expected me to be perfect, and if I didn't get things right, there would be consequences for the inconsistency of my performance. This conditioning caused me to look at God as my Lord, the One who expects me to do what He pleases, not the loving Father people talk about. It also caused me to go through life trying to please everyone and save everyone, even at the expense of my own mental and emotional health. I have learned I am a deep empath and this people-pleasing proclivity is called the fawn response. It is a trauma response, something I had no idea I was doing for years.

So, I see God as I saw my earthly father, sometimes compassionate and loving but then abusive and impossible to please. This perception of God has been a great struggle for me over the years, but I am thankful I have recognized this issue and am working through it. The struggle is real. It is challenging to believe God is a loving Father who listens and desires to answer my prayers instead of one who is looking and allowing me to suffer because I have not performed well enough to receive His goodness.

Evaluate the reasons for your feelings of doubt towards God. Why do you believe what you believe about Him and your situation? We always have to find the root of our beliefs and issues. Many times, people attack the fruit of their problems and are unaware the root is what is causing the belief or action. For years, I stopped asking God to do great things in my life and pursuing my goals because of ongoing disappointment from God. I didn't realize I felt rejected by God. The disappointment was the fruit, but the root was the feeling of rejection. I was conditioned to believe love and acceptance were performance-based, so I thought God was closing His ear and His hand to me.

Of course, this is not the truth. The truth is, God always hears me, and my performance is not predicated on God's goodness towards me. If I am going to know Him as my Father, I have to choose to believe God is who He said He is. God wants us to believe in Him, to have faith in Him and His goodness towards us. It is all about the posture of our hearts with God.

Truthfully, we will never be able to keep every commandment of God faithfully. Why, because we are incapable of it. We are all flawed, broken and full of sin. God knew this since the beginning though; when He created the first man Adam, which is why, He sent the last Adam, Jesus Christ. (1 Corinthians 15:45). God knows and understands the nature of our flesh. He knows it is a struggle for us at times to do what is right. Even the little things like, trusting His goodness.

The apostle Paul put it this way. "For I do not understand what I am doing, because I do not practice what I want to do, but I do what I hate." (Romans 7:15) Wow! The great apostle Paul is keeping it real about his struggle with the flesh. Paul understood that sinning was to go against the Spirit, and to go against God. Paul knew his struggles and limitations but he also had a desire to please God. (Romans 7: 16-25) Our desire to please God, is what God wants. When we have that deep desire to please and follow God, our hearts are in the right posture. God is never expecting perfection from us.

I think about David.

"After removing him, he raised up David as their king and testified about him: 'I have found David the son of Jesse to be a man after my own heart, who will carry out all my will'" (Acts 13:22).

David was called "a man after God's heart," but not because he was perfect. He was far from it. We are talking about the same guy who slept with his soldier Uriah's wife, got her pregnant, and had Uriah killed to cover up his sin (2 Samuel 11:1-12:9). We say slept, but it was rape. Let's call it what it was. David saw Bathsheba bathing and began to lust for Bathsheba, and he sent for her. He sent for her intending to have sexual relations with another man's wife. And no one had better turn down the king and his authority in those times, especially a woman.

Isn't this mind-blowing? I know some of you who have never heard the story of David and Bathsheba may be saying, "What in the world? How is this dude considered a man after God's own heart with all of that foul, ratchet stuff he did?" As stated before, it is all about the posture of our hearts. God knew David loved Him and wanted to please Him. David wanted to fulfill the will of God. When we read about David, we see David was a worshiper. Second Samuel 6:14 mentions how David worshiped the Lord with all his might. David loved God but was flawed and broken, just as we are.

I'm not saying we have committed sinful acts similar to David's, nor am I giving him a pass, but I am saying we are imperfect and sinful. Before we move ahead, let me point out that David did have to face the consequences of those sins he committed. Just as David had to face the consequences of his sin, we face the consequences for ours, but this has nothing to do with us being perfect or imperfect. It is just the principle of sowing and reaping.

My middle child has her license and is driving now. She recently received a ticket for going three miles over the speed limit in a school zone. So we graced her and told her she had to be more careful. Her dad and I graced her, but there was still a consequence. We had to pay a fine, and she received a scheduled court date. That made her very nervous because she had never been in trouble outside of home, not even in detention at school. She also had to take a class to keep that ticket off her driving record.

We graced our daughter and loved her through that mistake, but you better believe if sister-girl messes up again, we will take those car keys away from her indefinitely! We love her enough to correct her wrongs and protect her and others. God feels this way about us, too. He wants to protect us and teach us to do and be better. He doesn't want perfection but wants us to seek holiness and relationship with Him. We will never be perfect. We should always strive to be better, but while we remain in these sinful bodies, we will never reach the perfection of God. That, my friend, is the truth.

"For you are saved by grace through faith, and this is not from yourselves; it is God's gift not from works, so that no one can boast" (Ephesians 2:8-9).

We have to spend time with God in prayer and studying His Word. The more time we spend with God, the more it helps us to discern what is true and what is a lie. The Word of God tells us in John 8:32 that the truth shall set you free. We have to know the truth about God and ourselves. We have to be transparent and honest about what we believe, too, then we will be able to experience the healing and growth God wants us to walk in.

Who are you struggling to believe God is to you? It's okay; you don't have to be afraid to admit you are struggling, hurting, and doubting God. I know some of our sisters and brothers in the church have made people feel like they are wrong for expressing their true feelings about their pain and their struggle to believe in God. Don't allow this wrong mindset to keep you held in captivity. Being honest about our feelings and struggles is the key to freedom and healing. God is listening. God cares about us, my friend.

"O Lord, Listen to my cry for help. Pay attention to my prayer, for it comes from honest lips" (Psalm 17:1).

Sometimes, it can feel like God is not listening to our prayers. It can feel like our prayers are hitting the ceiling and going nowhere. Sometimes, it can feel like God is far away. Sometimes, you cannot muster the words because of deep sorrow and disappointment, like I have experienced many times. When this happens, don't stop communicating with God. Even if you have to do it in tears, keep praying. Even your groans mean something to the Lord. He understands them. God is listening and desires to have an open dialogue with you.

I have had my fair share of groans. There were times when I would go to God in tears, and the pain felt so severe all I could do was say, "Lord, HELP ME, Lord, HELP ME" while sobbing. These moments of sobbing have happened several times throughout my life, and I am sure they will happen again. Why? Because we will continue to have trials in this world. Jesus told His disciples they would face trouble, and so will we.

"I have told you these things so that in me you may have peace. You will have suffering in this world. Be courageous! I have conquered the world" (John 16:33).

My friend, we will surely experience suffering and pain. We will find ourselves groaning in the place of words due to the intense pain we may feel, but here is what it says in Romans 8:26-27.

> In the same way, the Spirit helps us in our weakness because we do not know what to pray for as we should, but the Spirit himself intercedes for us with unspoken groanings. And he who searches our hearts knows the mind of the Spirit because he intercedes for the saints according to the will of God.

So, even when we are mute of words to utter to God, in despair, and letting out cries of deep sorrow, those moanings and groanings are counted as words to our loving Father. He hears them, understands them, and will respond to them. Please believe that! God cares for and loves you. No matter what it feels like or looks like, God is right there with you in your situation. He is not listening, looking, and allowing you to suffer for His enjoyment. I know it feels like that sometimes. God is not finding joy in watching you hurt or struggle to make it through your trial, but He is finding joy in watching you stand in the victory He has given you over the enemy. God is always moving and doing something behind the scenes. It may not seem like it, but it's true. God works in us, for us, and through us if we allow Him to.

The pain we experience is never wasted with God. I'll say that again. Our pain is never wasted. Never! Shout that out in those times of frustration to silence the enemy and remind yourself that your suffering is not in vain. Make sure you are not in public somewhere when you perform this outburst; you don't want to look like a crazy person! But seriously, God has a plan, even before encountering the problem. You may be surprised by your trials, but God is never surprised. He already knows what you will go through, and because of His love for you, He is already working it out for your good.

Here is what Romans 8:28 says, "We know that all things work together for the good of those who love God, we who are called according to His purpose." Now we see where the Word of God tells us all things will work for our good. Not some things, not a few things, but all things! Believing that everything will work for my good is unbelievable sometimes; trust me, I know. Many things have happened in my life, and are still happening now, where the question remains: How will this trial work for my good? Yes, it is running through my head while tears stream down my face.

I have come to realize, though, I have to keep moving forward in the pain. I have to lean into God even more. Just as I have to press, I want to encourage you to do the same, my friend. Keep praying, pushing, and exercising your God-given patience so you can see the whole picture. Don't give up just yet. Wait to turn the movie off because the ending is beautiful!

The whole picture is something the enemy hates for us to see. He loves for us to give up before we can receive the promises of God. But we can't receive the promises of God without the process. Process equals the promises of God. Just as gold has to go through a refining process to be free of impurities, this is the case for the people of God. God is our heavenly, holy Goldsmith, refining our character for His glory. Just as the olive has to go through the crushing for oil production, we have to experience crushing to produce what God is trying to bring out of us.

As the potter molds his clay into what he envisions, our heavenly Father molds us into who He created us to become. He is the potter, and we are His clay. God uses the ugly twists and turns of life's trials and challenges to improve us. We are His beautiful mess He molds into His perfection. God is always making us better. The goal is for us to become more like Him.

The refining process is the top priority for God. The answers to our prayers are a bonus, or shall I say, if you are a Louisiana native, it's *lagniappe*! The process comes first and promises second. God wants our character to have the capacity to handle what He is entrusting us with. So, go through the process and wait for the promise. Yes, the process hurts greatly! I am in the process now, and it hurts deeply, but I am doing my best to stay focused on the promise so the process doesn't turn me away from God and destroy me.

15

Chapter 2
Keep Praising In The Process

P raise: To worship, commend, or give honor to (HCSB).

In Psalm 144:1-5, David, the author of this psalm, is rejoicing in God in the good and bad times. God desires us to bless and praise Him at all times, just as David did. But praising God is one of the most challenging things to do during hard times, especially when you feel like He is allowing you to go through or stay in a difficult situation.

Indeed, we must do this by faith, not by what we see or feel. Yes, I know you are thinking or saying to yourself as you read this, "REALLY? YOU DON'T KNOW ALL THE HELL I AM EXPERIENCING RIGHT NOW! I NEED THIS TO CHANGE RIGHT NOW"! I get it, but I also want you to know praise is a weapon that empowers us to silence the roaring lies and accusations of the enemy. I honestly don't know what I would do without it. I sometimes praise God and silence the enemy by playing powerful praise or worship music, singing aloud to God, clapping, and sometimes even dancing around at home. Believe me when I say it works!

Music is powerful, and when coupled with the right spirit and words, it is fuel for our souls. The enemy tries to steal our praise because he realizes it gets us out of our stupor. When we praise God wholeheartedly, we are no longer confused about His goodness toward us.

Even if we still have not received an answer from God at that moment, our spirits become lifted, and we can continue on our journey. Weeping may stay overnight, but there is joy in the morning (Psalm 30:5). Your morning can be in seconds, minutes, hours, days, weeks, or even months. It's totally up to you when you want to receive joy.

I am not saying you should not process the pain if you are grieving a loss, are experiencing deep hurt from some type of trauma, or even feel discouraged by waiting on God for something. By all means, please do so. Sit in those emotions and feel them, voice them, and process them. It is all about being emotionally healthy, coupled with spiritual health. Processing your feelings is the path to healing and restoration. Some people do not understand this concept because they are used to sweeping things under the rug and moving on, not even realizing this is unhealthy behavior.

The problem with this behavior is the pain they are sweeping under the rug is affecting them and significantly affecting the people around them and their relationship with God. That pain is still present. They may believe they are fine, but their behaviors show otherwise. They may be storing pent-up anger or depression and may not even realize it is because they have not processed their trauma. If you know someone like this, please pray the eyes of their understanding will be enlightened so they can heal properly.

You also may consider staying away from this individual while you are trying to process your pain to experience the true healing you seek.

I say this because people with this mindset will say or even do the wrong things and not give you the care and compassion you need. We need to be in life-giving, safe environments when we are healing. We need to stay away from people who will add to our trauma or keep us from healing from it. We need to be around people who will bring us healing and life. So, process your pain correctly, but also, please remember to rely on the Lord to bring you out of that pain and heal you. True, lasting healing only comes from Him. I am a living witness to that. Many people can experience behavior modification; they can act a certain way for a while, but true deep internal healing only comes through the power of God. So, praise God today. Put on some music and silence the enemy. Offer up the incense of praise to God with your words by faith, even if they are few.

As stated before, I know this can be challenging when you feel heavy and weighed down. If you have to get up each day and try and try, then do that. If you have to lie in bed and listen to music with tears streaming down your face as you clap your hands, then do that. If you have to call friends over to have a praise party while you watch them jump around looking silly to make you laugh, then do that. Wow! I can just picture in my head right now my friends dancing around acting silly to cheer me up. Trust me, my friends are quite the characters. I love it, though, and I love them dearly! The Bible says "a joyful heart is good medicine, but a broken spirit dries up the bones" (Proverbs 17:22). Cry if you must, but don't let the enemy take your praise. Praise is powerful and helps us rejoice in those hard times.

The enemy is always after our praise. The enemy doesn't want us to praise God. He wants us to curse God. Stealing Job's joy was a part of the enemy's plan. He ultimately wanted Job's faith, though. Let's look at what it says in Job chapter 1:9-11.

> Satan answered the Lord, "Does Job fear God for nothing? Haven't You placed a hedge around him, his household, and everything he owns? You have blessed the works of his hands, and his possessions have increased in the land. But stretch out your hand and strike everything he owns, and he will surely curse you to your face."

Indeed, it is all about making us turn away from God. Satan wants to steal our praise. He wants to kill our faith. In those tough times, it is easy to turn away from God, to stay silent, and not give God praise or acknowledge His goodness. Remember the enemy is a liar and a thief. Don't let him lie to you by telling you God doesn't love you. Don't let him tell you God is holding out on you. Satan used this tactic on Eve in the garden.

Here is what went down.

> Now the serpent was the most cunning of all the wild animals that the Lord God had made. He said to the woman."Did God really say, 'You can't eat from any tree in the garden'"? The woman said to the serpent, "We may eat the fruit from the trees in the garden. But about the fruit of the tree in the middle of the garden, God said, 'You must not eat it or touch it, or you will die." "No! You will not die," the serpent said to the woman. "In fact, God knows that when you eat it your eyes will be opened and you will be like God, knowing good and evil." The woman saw that the tree was good for food and delightful to look at, and that it was desirable for obtaining wisdom. So she took some of its fruit and ate it; she also gave some to her husband and he ate it. Then the eyes of them were opened, and they knew they were naked; so they sewed fig leaves together and made coverings for themselves (Genesis 3:1-7).

Satan was able to lie to Eve by telling her she was not like God, when the truth is, she was. In Genesis 1:26-27, God says He made man in His image and likeness. He created male and female this way. He also blessed them.

I am continuing to see how the enemy will always try to get us to believe we are not who God said we are and that we cannot have what He has already blessed us with. For example, God has already blessed us with His peace.

"Peace I leave with you. My peace I give to you. I do not give to you as the world gives. Don't let your heart be troubled or fearful" (John 14:27).

Satan will never stop trying to persuade people to believe his lies. Now, let us jump back into the text. Satan also made Eve think God was holding out on her, but the enemy deceived her by getting her to pay attention to the one thing God told her she couldn't have, which was for her protection. Satan lied to her. But when the lie didn't work, he told her a half-truth.

We, too, can allow the enemy to get us focused on the things we can't have while forgetting all we do have. Sometimes, God wants to give us what we want if we can wait patiently, enjoy life, and praise Him in the process. Patience is something we all struggle with. James 1 mentions the production of patience in us: "And let patience have his perfect work, that you may be perfect and complete, lacking nothing" (James 1:4). So, we see that patience makes us complete. So, why do we fight it? Don't we want to be complete?

You may be saying to yourself, "Of course I want to be complete." Many of us want to be made complete, but we want it without going through the pain. Who loves pain? No one in their right mind does. We want to avoid it at all costs. For me, sometimes I feel like I have gone through enough pain. Sometimes, I ask God, can you do whatever you need to do in me without pain? Then, I find myself praying to be more like Jesus. I ask God to take everything that does not please Him out of me. Lord, am I crazy or what? But I know God can only strip us of fleshly behaviors through trials. These trials reveal our hearts and minds and cause us to seek Him for answers and relief. As we seek God for answers and relief, it draws us closer to Him. We will always experience some type of pain because we live in a fallen world, and we have an enemy who is always looking to devour us—an enemy who wants to take us out.

James 1 also mentions we should count it all joy when we fall into various trials and that the testing of faith produces patience in us (James 1:2). So, the testing of our faith produces patience. The development of patience is making us complete. The scripture also tells us to be joyful, not about the trial itself but about the growth the trial produces in us. Do you know the Greek word for *joy* in James 1:2, which is the word *chara*, is the same word used for the joy Jesus experienced regarding His crucifixion for our salvation? "Keeping our eyes on Jesus, the source and perfecter of our faith. For the joy that lay before him, he endured the cross, despising the shame, and sat down at the right hand at the throne of God" (Hebrews 12:2). Jesus found joy in knowing that through His suffering we would have salvation, and that He would be seated at the right hand of the throne of God.

Jesus remained focused because He kept His eyes on the purpose of the pain. We, too, can only stay focused by keeping our eyes on the purpose of our pain—developing our character and knowing one day we will go to heaven, where there will be no more suffering.

Hebrews 12:2 also mentions Jesus as the source and perfecter of our faith. So, we should all look to the Source of our faith, joy, peace, patience, strength, health, finances, and everything we need. We often forget to go to the Source, so we find ourselves frustrated, defeated, and lacking the joy God has already given us.

Lord knows I need help putting this into practice. I can see how busy my day will be, running errands, cleaning the house, and preparing a meal, and the limited time I have to squeeze it all in before checking my daughter out of school early to get her to her bowling matches. I can let all this run through my head and try to figure it out independently, never asking God how to get it all done first. The funny thing is I pray for direction in the morning when I wake up but never wait for Him to show me what that looks like. I just hit the ground running, and then I find myself overwhelmed. Which leads me to begin feeling like life is too hard. And there it is—I just gave my joy away because I didn't look to God, the Source, for help. Now, the overwhelming feeling of life has stolen not only my joy but also my praise. Once our joy has been stolen, we can no longer give God the praises He deserves. We find ourselves complaining instead.

Don't get me wrong, sometimes life can be overwhelming, but we can never forget to go to God for help. God is concerned about even the most minor details of our life. I used to pray for help, but many times after, I looked at everything on the list and tried to determine how to make it happen. Lord Jesus! Help a sister out! Your daughter Q needs help badly! I realized this independence is another bad habit from my childhood. I was conditioned to believe I always had to be in charge and responsible for things. But I can see the error of my ways now. Praise be to God! God is perfecting me, and I will keep praising Him for that. Hallelujah!

Chapter 3
I'm Trying To Adore Him

Adoration is adoring, worshiping, and honoring a deity or divine.

(Psalm 104:1-35) The anonymous author appreciates God for His creation and the maintenance of His creation.

(Job 37: 1-24) Elihu reminds Job of God's power (Key verse: 24).

Because adoration is a form of worship, it can be hard to do when we are disappointed. Sometimes we ask ourselves, *why would I worship a God who doesn't even hear or care about me?* We can feel like God is not concerned about our struggles, hurts, or dreams. Every follower of Christ battles these feelings. Sometimes, it is hard to adore or even desire to draw close to someone you feel is not there for you.

I have struggled with this. I asked God years ago where He was in my marriage when I prayed for my husband to be more selfless and considerate. I asked where He was when I experienced years of sickness in my body and had no answers. I asked where He was when my mother died an hour before I could reach her to say goodbye. One hour—the same amount of time Jesus asked His disciples to pray with Him in His hour of agony. I wanted to look into her brown eyes and hold her warm hand while she held mine. I hoped to tell her I loved her and wanted to hear her say it to me one last time. I hoped to be able to do all these things and more but didn't get the opportunity. All that earnest prayer, and for what? Why, God?

I asked God where He was during the 2016 flood we experienced. I remember being so disappointed and feeling like God had abandoned me after earnestly praying for Him to keep my home from flooding—all this right after the hurt and disappointment of losing my mother in 2015. Well, our home not only flooded, it flooded with four feet of water, causing us to lose everything, including two vehicles; one of the vehicles we had canceled the insurance on because someone was about to purchase it from us. So we thought. We lost it all and found ourselves walking through the scary, infested flood waters with our two young daughters and teenage son. Thank God our girls had a little height on them. We were able to tiptoe through the flood waters and eventually found dry ground.

We later found ourselves walking, wondering how and where we would go. Thankfully, we were soon picked up by an off-duty firefighter, who took us to the nearest hotel. We thought we would have to sleep outside due to no hotel vacancies. The fireman walked back into the hotel and then came back to say how he managed to get us a room. We still don't know how he did it, but to this day, we know it was the Lord looking out for us. From there, all five of us spent the next three months cramped in a double-queen hotel room. It was frustrating, from fighting with the insurance company to get our funds to dealing with contractors who tried to milk us for money, all while living in that hotel room. After FEMA denied us assistance, my family and I were forced to move into our home while it was still being renovated. We had to store our clothes outside in an on-site storage rental.

That whole process, from start to finish, was stressful. I was also homeschooling my daughters during this time. On top of the stress, I felt abandoned and forgotten by God on many occasions, but I knew I had to keep praying to Him to strengthen me in the journey. I know it was His grace that got me and my family through that difficult time.

Deep pain can make us feel like there is nothing to worship God for. I am not saying this to sound inconsiderate—I am encouraging you to look carefully at your life in these moments. Ask God to help you do this. He will. Once you ask for His help with your broken heart, the key is to speak out by faith until your emotions follow. Get out of your head and let your spirit guide you. Keep speaking until you feel encouraged, strengthened, and desire to worship God. If I did not do what I am recommending, I would have lost my mind and hope in the possibility of good things from my trials.

We can adore God for many things, but sometimes, our trials are so weighty and can close our eyes to all the good things happening. Focus on who God is—His goodness, deity, and character. As you spend time with God today, write down all of His character traits in your journal so you can go back and reflect on His goodness and be reminded of them when you find yourself struggling. We are all conflicted at times, but it is okay. We're human. It's our nature. We will question the goodness of God and may even question who He is. Even John the Baptist struggled and questioned who Jesus was.

> "Now when John heard in prison what the Christ was doing, he sent a message through his disciples and asked him, "Are you the one who is to come, or should we look for another?" Jesus replied to them, "Go and report to John what you hear and see: The blind receive their sight, the lame walk, those with leprosy are cleansed, the deaf hear, the dead are raised, and the poor are told the good news, and blessed is the one who isn't offended by me" (Matthew 11:2-6).

Yes, John the Baptist, who prepared the way for Jesus, struggled with doubt in his season of hardship. So, don't beat yourself up when you wrestle to believe in God's goodness. God does not want us to beat up on ourselves about our shortcomings. His Word tells us not to do this. His Word is His words—Him speaking to us. Keep pressing to do better in this area and wherever you are struggling until you walk in the victory God has already given you.

"Therefore, there is no condemnation for those in Christ Jesus" (Romans 8:1).

Before we move on, I want to share those prayers for my husband to be more considerate have manifested. He was always a good-willed man of God, but now he is more God-willed, more sensitive to the things of God, to others, and even more in tune with himself. Prayer and working through some childhood trauma in therapy helped him reach that point. I love the man my husband has become, and I look forward to experiencing our continuous growth! It was so worth the wait!

I now have a second home. After staying in our home for a few years, we decided it was time to move. Instead of selling it, I decided to turn it into a rental property after talking to one of my dear friends about needing another source of income. God not only restored what we lost but gave us double. Praise God! We didn't see it at the time of the loss, but God worked something good out of our pain.

Lastly, my struggle with my health is still present. I am not where I would like to be, but I thank God I am not where I was. Where it was hard for me to function a lot of the time, I am experiencing less of that now. I have more good days than bad ones. Where we couldn't find what was wrong with me, now we have a diagnosis after many years of searching and seeing many doctors and specialists. My new gynecologist figured it out—it's an autoimmune disorder, in case your nosey side is wondering. But in all seriousness, I wanted to share the outcome of these issues to encourage you to keep praying and pressing and giving God the adoration He deserves, no matter what.

Let me also share with you this before we move on to the next chapter. I am grateful to have discovered what I am carrying in my body. I may not have experienced the fullness of the healing I am praying for, but God has healed my stomach, liver, gallbladder, and kidney, which were close to declining. My stomach had no healthy bacteria at all. Those proton pump inhibitors, which the doctor shouldn't have prescribed to me, had done a massive number on my gut. The ignorance and negligence of the gastro doctor caused my gut to become severely damaged.

The medicine suppressed the acid in my stomach so much that it caused digestive issues for me and allowed parasites to creep in. My immune system had become highly weakened because of the lack of healthy bacteria, and about 80 percent of the immune system stems from the gut. I had to rebuild a healthy gut microbiome with gut-healing foods and supplements. My God, the journey!

I was angry at the doctors and angry at God, because He allowed me to go through it. When I started my journey of research on healing, I had no idea where to begin. I cried many days and felt hopeless, but I was desperate, so I kept searching until I found the answers. It took months to find those answers but thank God I did. The healing process did not happen overnight, either. It took years to see the progress I am now experiencing. It also took lots of prayer, discipline, and perseverance.

As heartbreaking and challenging as this was, I have gained a wealth of knowledge on the body, essential oils, supplements, foods, and natural remedies. People are amazed when they hear me say I do not own any type of headache or pain medicine or any stomach and allergy medicine. Nor do I take any prescription drugs for my autoimmune disorder. I just use natural remedies for all of these issues. My family uses natural remedies as well.

My situation may be challenging and can cause me discomfort some days. Still, I have gained so much from going through it and have been able to help others prevent things from happening or becoming worse in their bodies. For this, my friend, I am very grateful and have to give God the adoration He deserves.

Chapter 4
Confession, So Good For The Soul

Confession—to acknowledge, agree, admit something; profession or to openly express.

"Brothers and sisters, my heart's desire and prayer to God concerning them is for their salvation" (Romans 10:1).

"And I say to you, anyone who acknowledges me before others, the Son of Man will acknowledge him before the angels of God, but whoever denies me before others will be denied before the angels of God. Anyone who speaks blasphemes against the Holy Spirit will not be forgiven" (Luke 12:8-10).

In Matthew 3:1-6, John the Baptist was calling people to repentance. This work was his God-giving assignment, his purpose. We all have one, but if we never give our lives to Jesus Christ, our Lord and Savior, which requires true heart-aligned repentance, we will never know or walk in our divine assignment. So, if you do not know Jesus, I encourage you to take this time to confess your sins to God and ask Him to come into your life and help you live the life He desires to give you. That life is a life full of the abundance of God! "A thief comes only to steal and kill and destroy. I have come so that they may have life and have it in abundance" (John 10:10).

Even when we turn our lives over to Jesus, we still need to ask for forgiveness for the sins we may commit, because we are sinful by nature. Prayerfully, we become more conscious about our sins with time and growth and are quick to repent and turn away from those destructive behaviors. When we are quick to repent and ask God for forgiveness, it helps eliminate the question of whether our prayers are being hindered or if we are being punished for our sins. God always wants to hear and answer our prayers according to His will. Knowing this truth is why we should always be willing and ready to repent. God is not just sitting and waiting to punish you, but we suffer the consequences of our actions.

If someone enters a bank, robs it, kills a few people doing it, and gets caught by the authorities, he will face the consequences for those crimes. We have to know this principle is the same spiritually as it is naturally. We will experience the ramifications of our willful acts of sin. I often tell my children that if we want to reap a good harvest, we must do our best to sow good seeds.

Here is what the Word says: "Don't be deceived: God is not mocked. For whatever a person sows he will also reap, because the one who sows to his flesh will reap destruction from the flesh, but the one who sows to the Spirit will reap eternal life from the Spirit" (Galatians 6:7-8). BAM, it's right there in the text. You reap what YOU sow. Hold up there, na, don't look at me in that tone of voice while saying, "Okay, what about the people who are innocent and go through?" I feel you; I got you. I am in no way saying everything wrong that happens to people is a consequence of their actions. I know we sometimes suffer the consequences of others' actions, too. We suffer due to someone else's sinful choices. This unfortunate truth happens often, too.

For instance, many of the unarmed African-American men police falsely accused of being violent and non-compliant were shot and killed, and their families suffered because of someone else's sinful act of racism and hate. The girl who is raped by her relative is suffering at the hands of that person's immoral perverted act. There are countless ways individuals suffer from someone else's choices. I often hear people say, if God is so good, why is He allowing all the bad in the world? That goes back to my statement about our destructive, sinful nature. God has given us all free will. He is not going to take it back. Because we have a nature to sin, those who have not yielded their lives over to God are easily influenced by the enemy.

The man who does not have some actual mental illness and goes into the school or church to open fire on innocent people has possibly surrendered himself to the devil. The man who is kidnapping women and children and selling them into sex slavery has yielded to the devil. The man who has violated and raped a woman has yielded to the enemy. The woman who sells her children for drugs has surrendered to the enemy.

All these things are happening because individuals are sowing to their flesh. Their natureis sinful, and they have not connected to the One who can help them develop a new nature.

In Psalm 51:5, David speaks about how he was sinful when his mother conceived him. So, from the womb, we are sinful. Think about it. A four-year-old does not need to be taught to lie about taking a cookie from the cookie jar without permission. Why? Because lying is in his nature.

God is not sinful, but we are. Our sinful nature is why we need God's saving grace to help us walk in His righteousness. We also need a wise community of believers who can challenge us when we do something contrary to a holy lifestyle. We need individuals who will help us walk in the righteousness of God.

We need people who care enough to be honest with us because they understand the importance of life-giving truth. We also have the Holy Spirit, who empowers us to walk upright. But all this starts with our confession and acknowledgment.

First John 1:9 states, "If we confess our sins, He is faithful and righteous to forgive us our sins and to cleanse us from all unrighteousness." My God! This verse is so powerful! It does not matter what type of sin we may have committed, whether it be abortion, unforgiveness, or false witness; if we repent for our actions and ask God to forgive us, He does and cleanses us from all our sins. All means all, so not some, not a little, but *all* our sins. He makes us new. That is something to celebrate! GLORY TO GOD!

Don't let guilt and shame keep you from asking God for forgiveness. The enemy likes to use our past to keep us bound and away from the presence of God. In Psalm 32, David speaks of the joy of forgiveness. It is a beautiful thing to receive forgiveness from the Lord. Receiving forgiveness helps us let go of the heavy baggage we carry around with us. When we receive forgiveness from God, we realize Jesus has already paid the penalty for our sins. Therefore, we no longer have to carry the weight of them.

When we receive God's forgiveness, the enemy can no longer torment us about our past or future sins. We learn how to embrace and enjoy the journey called life. We understand God loves us, and our imperfections have nothing to do with His love for us. We also learn how to love ourselves, even with all our imperfections, because we know the Holy Spirit is working in us to bring transformation into our lives.

Receiving the forgiveness of God also allows us to be willing to forgive others. Why? We recognize that God has freely forgiven us and that He could have chosen not to. Holding on to unforgiveness is also hurting us. Carrying unforgiveness can open a door for sickness to enter our bodies. Unforgiveness can rob us of joy and peace and steal life from us. We walk around holding on to what the person did to us while that person has gone on with their life, but we are suffering. No, thank you, devil. I'll take forgiveness instead.

Sometimes, we hold on to what people have done to us because we may believe if we let the offense go, we somehow let them get away with what they have done. Sometimes, we hold on to the offense because we feel we need some type of apology from the wrongdoer to move forward. In cases like this, it may be best to speak with a licensed therapist to move forward, someone trained to help you figure out why you cannot escape that rut of unforgiveness.

Sometimes, we may have difficulty forgiving ourselves because we allowed someone to hurt us and did not stand up for ourselves. We allowed ourselves to be taken advantage of, manipulated, controlled, and bullied. I am working through this process of forgiving myself in therapy now. I was so angry for allowing myself to be bullied and controlled some years ago by a few individuals. I know God will help me get past this and heal eventually. God does not want me to hold on to what happened to me and how I was not emotionally healthy enough to set boundaries. He understands. God does not want us to harbor unforgiveness towards others or ourselves. He desires us to process our hurts but not hold them in our hearts.

If you are battling unforgiveness, confess it to Jesus and ask Him to help you conquer it. He will step in and help you to forgive. I also want you to know God is not happy about what happened to you, and He will repay that person for the wrong they have committed against you. I can't promise you that you will see that person's consequences, but I can say they will experience them. Romans 12:19 says, "Friends, do not avenge yourselves; instead, leave room for God's wrath, because it is written, 'Vengeance belongs to me; I will repay, says the Lord.'"

Yes, God will repay people for their wrongs toward us, but we should never look for it to happen. We always want to ensure our hearts are free and clear of hate. God desires us to have pure hearts. So, if you hope to see your wrongdoer suffer, confess that as a sin, ask for forgiveness, and pray for that person. Also, pray you will always desire to have a repentant heart that is quick to repent but also quick to forgive.

Again, I am not teaching the whole "shove your feelings aside or under the rug" when I say pray to forgive quickly. There may be times when the desire to forgive may be challenging due to a great offense, like rape. It may take years for that individual to feel forgiving toward their offender. I can understand that, too. They need that time.

Some of our church communities have damaged individuals with this "shove your feelings" approach. This mindset is why we have so many people whose hearts are hard towards other people and, sadly, towards God. They believe many emotions are wrong and ungodly. They won't allow themselves or others to process sadness, fear, disappointment, anger, or any other emotion that does not express joy or peace. Expressing any other feeling besides these is showing a lack of faith.

I have encountered individuals who made me feel like expressing my feelings was wrong. I am not talking about sinfully expressing my emotions and being corrected. I am talking about moments when I was hurting so badly, and I expressed my hurt. These individuals quoted scripture and said they would pray I would be strong instead of allowing me to be human, process my pain, and then comfort me with a hug or some form of affection. Of course, I love scripture and prayer, but the "be strong" scripture should come after the comfort. Unfortunately, this is a massive issue in many churches.

Lord, help Your church see, grasp, and embrace the truth about feelings, emotions, and mental health. I firmly believe that when the body of Christ gets this understanding, the church will become that church God is coming for, the church without spot or blemish. We will become healthier when we deal with emotions healthily, especially our own. The crazy things we deal with in the church, like jealousy, slander, and gossip, would be less messy if we could understand, interpret, process, and express emotions better. Let's not forget emotions are throughout the entire Bible. Even Jesus expressed emotions. When He was praying in the Garden of Gethsemane, Jesus experienced and expressed sorrow and fear.

"Then Jesus came with them to a place called Gethsemane, and he told the disciples, 'Sit here while I go over there and pray.' Taking along Peter and the two sons of Zebedee, he began to be sorrowful and troubled. He said to them, 'I am deeply grieved to the point of death. Remain here and stay awake with me.' Going a little farther, he fell face down and prayed, 'My Father, if it is possible, let this cup pass from me. Yet not as I will, but as you will'" (Matthew 26:36-39).

We also see in verses 42 and 44 where Jesus prayed the same prayer two more times. Luke 22:44 says the weight of anguish on Jesus' body caused Him to sweat drops of blood. So, if Jesus expressed great pain and fear, why do some believe we shouldn't express pain and fear? Why have we embraced this lie when the Truth is speaking? Well, today, I am sounding the alarm. Stop hurting people with lies about emotions.

Expressing our feelings is not sinful. It makes God look unloving and out of touch with us. How do we pray to a God who does not care about our feelings? Stop and ponder on that for a second. If my feelings don't matter, why would God respond to me regarding them? Can you imagine not responding to your child when they are hurting? I don't know of any loving parent who would not come to the aid or rescue of their child in those times if they can. I know as a mother, I want to keep my children from hurting as much as possible. I always want to protect them. I hate to see them stressed, frustrated, worried, sick, or injured, and I definitely hate to see them cry. I sometimes find myself thinking, *if I can love my children this much, then how much more can God love me?* God cares about my pain and wants to come to my aid too. My pain matters to Him. This can be hard to remember at times, but it is true. God notices the welling up in my eyes and the knot in my throat when my body responds to my emotions. Yes, He notices every tear streaming down my face.

"You yourself have recorded my wanderings. Put my tears in your bottle. Are they not in your book?" (Psalm 56:8).

I believe God gave us emotions to evaluate where we are and to show us what's in our hearts. God also wants us to express our feelings healthily, process them, and have great relationships with Him and others through healthy emotions. He also wants others to know where we are and how their behaviors have affected us, whether bad or good. I am praying people will receive this truth. If you have not received this truth yet, please do so now.

Regarding forgiveness, when someone has wronged you, the first thing to do is tell God how you feel and ask Him to help you forgive this person quickly. From there, you pray for yourself, for the wrongdoer, and process the hurt to get to the healing part. If you feel sad, afraid, or frustrated, say it. Sit in those feelings; don't avoid or run from them. We should always process our feelings. Always. No matter what feeling it is. Process them, and let God heal you from the hurt causing those emotions. We can only move forward if we confess how we feel, where we are, and what we have done first. We have to be honest about where we are to receive the change and healing God desires to give us. Yes, confession is so good for the soul! Taste and see, my friend! You will not be disappointed. There is true liberty and peace in it.

Chapter 5
I Don't Feel Thankful

Thanksgiving—A prayer expressing gratitude, a public acknowledgment, or a celebration of God's goodness.

"Give thanks in everything; for this is God's will for you in Christ Jesus" (1 Thessalonians 5:18).

(Psalm 92:1-6) It is a Psalm used in the temple services on the Sabbath.

There are times we do not feel thankful, even when we know Psalm 92 says it is good to thank the Lord. How do we give thanks in everything, as 1 Thessalonians 5:18 tells us to? Occasionally, our problems will cause us, myself included, not to be thankful. I am fighting to feel thankful as I am writing this book. Why? Because we are facing many hardships. On top of that, several people have done unjust things, some of which involved taking money from us over the years without repercussions. Some have even turned away from and mistreated us because of our belief and stance for righteousness and truth, but I have decided to cast my care.

Our mind can sometimes take us to places we should not go. We can find ourselves stuck in a negative rut, thinking about all the bad things happening in our lives. I am a worrier by nurture and nature. I can be very melancholy at times, especially when my hormones are out of whack. I have improved at controlling my thoughts over the years, though. I used to let negative thoughts pile up on me. They would roll over and over in my mind. Any thought the enemy offered me, I received it and meditated on it. Lord Jesus! Rehearsing these negative thoughts caused me to become overwhelmed and defeated. I would allow my thoughts to take me deep into a pit, and then I would have to work extra hard to try to escape it. The hard work happened because I didn't work the Word of God or even understand the root cause of all my worries.

Philippians 4:6 says, "Don't worry about anything, but in everything, through prayer and petition with thanksgiving, present your request to God." But wait, it doesn't stop there: Philippians 4:7 tells us what will happen if we do what verse 6 tells us to do. It reads, "And the peace of God, that surpasses all understanding, will guard your hearts and minds in Christ Jesus."

Finally, verse 8 tells us what to replace negative thought patterns with.

"Finally, brothers and sisters, whatever is true, whatever is honorable, whatever is just, whatever is pure, whatever is lovely, whatever is commendable—if there is any moral excellence and if there is anything praiseworthy—dwell on these things."

The Word of God is giving us the weapon to defeat those negative thoughts, but we must use it. These verses in Philippians 4 are some of the verses I use to keep my mind from being filled with negative thoughts. My sister and I have developed a saying we jokingly but seriously use: "You're offering, but I ain't receiving, Satan." I know that is not proper English, but I AIN'T RECEIVING, devil! On the flip side, I understand some individuals have clinical issues, like imbalances with their brain, and need professional help. If this is you, don't try to do it alone. Please! Get professional help if you need it.

As for those of us who just struggle with negative thought patterns, we must have the right people surrounding us to help us remain thankful. That is why having a church community is necessary. Being around positivity and love can help us defeat that spirit of negativity that sometimes creeps in unannounced. You don't want to hang around a negative Nancy who keeps you in your negative rut. (If your name is Nancy, and you are reading this—sorry! Your name flows well with *negative*.) We need to surround ourselves with positive people. As the song says, "There's Joy in the House of the Lord"! There is. I can recall when I did not feel like going to church or being around people, but when I arrived, my whole attitude changed because of the love and positivity I encountered. A friendly hug at the door as I arrived, even the smile as I approached the church entrance, helped uplift my spirit.

I remember starting "thankful mornings" with my daughters while I took them to school. I wanted them to learn to appreciate what God had given them daily, training them and instilling something in them they would need for the rest of their lives. I know how easy it can be for us all to complain and not be grateful for what we have.

At first, it was hard for them to think about what to be grateful for, but it became more natural as time passed. It also made them see how they took so many things for granted. Does that sound familiar? I know you are nodding and saying, "Oh, Lord, yes."

We have all been there. Time and time again, around the same mountain we go. You know what is crazy? When we read about the children of Israel, in Exodus 15:22-27 and 16:1-12, we quickly see how they are complaining but don't realize when *we* are complaining. Complaining gets us nowhere. We end up staying in some of our situations longer. It's all about God maturing us and teaching us how to have true joy. Genuine joy is never predicated on what we have or how we feel. Absolute joy can only take place when we remain thankful.

We can find ourselves trying to discover what we are grateful for. We can become so complacent and spoiled by our luxuries. We can act like little ingrates. Forgive us, Jesus. The good thing about this, though, is God understands and graces us. Thank God for His unfailing grace! Where would we ever be without it?

Chapter 6
Keep Making Your Request

Supplication—a request, plea for mercy, to humbly ask for something.

"Do not be anxious about anything, but in every situation, by prayer and petition with thanksgiving, present your request to God" (Philippians 4:6).

It can seem pointless to ask for something when you feel God is not there for you. It can be hard to request something from a God who appears to be never-present instead of ever-present. Maybe you feel forsaken, abandoned, rejected, or forgotten. I am in a season where I have been feeling like this. I feel like, "God, where are you? What are you doing? What are you saying? Where am I going?" I feel downright confused.

I can honestly and transparently say I struggle with feeling rejected and abandoned by God when He is silent in my place of turmoil and waiting. I have realized this mindset is due to the abandonment, rejection, and abuse I experienced from loved ones as a young child. Having gone through these types of issues, I attend therapy to ensure I am emotionally healthy.

We have to get the emotional healing we need to have the abundant life God desires us to have. When we are not emotionally and mentally whole, it causes us to view God and healthy loving relationships through distorted lenses. We do not want to live this way, and God doesn't want us to.

Confusion can be an ongoing struggle for every Christian. Wrestling with confusion is okay, but when it causes us to question God's character and love for us, this is an unhealthy, distorted view. I believe God allows confusion to happen so we can exercise our faith and deepen our relationship with Him. In the Gospel of Matthew 28:20, Jesus told the disciples He would be with them always. This promise also applies to us. God is always with us, even when we can't see or feel it. This guessing game of trying to figure out where God is and what He is doing reminds me of the song "Way Maker" by Sinach, the song's original writer. (There is a fun fact for you. You're welcome!)

The song's bridge says, "Even when I don't see it, You're working. Even when I don't feel it, You're working. You never stop. You never stop working." It is a powerful reminder of who God is and how He is always moving behind the scenes in our lives. This is why we have to continue making our requests to God. Like the parable Jesus told His disciples of the persistent widow in Luke 18, we must continue to pray.

Here's what it says:

Now he told them a parable on the need for them to pray always and not give up. There was a judge in a certain town who didn't fear God or respect people. And a widow in that town kept coming to him, saying, "Give me justice against my adversary." For a while he was unwilling, but later he said to himself, "Even though I don't fear God or respect people, yet because this widow keeps pestering me, I will give her justice, so that she doesn't wear me out by her persistent coming." Then the Lord said, "Listen to what the unjust judge says. Will not God grant justice to his elect who cry out to him day and night? Will he delay helping them? I tell you that he will swiftly grant them justice. Nevertheless, when the Son of Man comes, will he find faith on earth?" (Luke 18:1-8).

We have to continue to pray when we don't see anything happening. We have to be persistent. We have to pray day and night, believing God will grant us justice over our adversary, the devil. Our persistent prayers show our tenacious faith in God, giving us access to what our Heavenly Father has for us. Before we can make a plea or request, we must humble ourselves. We have to see and trust the sovereignty of God, knowing His plans are perfect for us. His no, delays, and yes are all working for our good.

Many times, He grants us the things we ask for if we just surrender and trust in Him instead of trying to force something to happen ourselves.

We do this a lot of the time because we find ourselves operating in the spirit of entitlement. We believe we deserve what we are asking for, so God had better answer us and answer quickly! This attitude will cause us to wait longer because God wants us to develop patience and be grateful and selfless.

We live in a time when everything is about getting everything fast. How to lose weight fast, how to learn to play an instrument fast, how to grow your hair fast, everything fast, fast, fast. We even want our food quickly and then complain when it isn't hot, but we don't have the patience to wait for the fresh batch of fries or chicken, which we shouldn't be eating anyway. I'm just saying. We even swallow too fast without chewing our food enough, and we wonder why so many people have digestive issues. We are moving quickly, never settling down to rest, and causing stress on our bodies. We have to realize waiting can be good sometimes.

I have had to teach this to my kids several times. They are so accustomed to having their needs, as well as some of their wants, met immediately. Experiencing this sometimes causes them to think that whenever they want something, it needs to happen ASAP! I remind them life is about more than getting what they want when they want. As hard as it may be for them to wait, they must trust my wisdom and love to make the right decisions for them.

This is exactly how God feels about us. If only we could get it, though. I honestly don't know if we will ever let God do what He wants in His timing without it being a struggle for us. Ohhh, the flesh desires what it wants. Lol! Lots of the time. It wants what it wants. I urge you to wait on the timing of God, though. PLEASE!

I can't let you leave this chapter without reading about at least one of my persistent prayer stories. As I stated earlier, I have an autoimmune disorder. It took many years to figure this out. My husband and I searched and searched for answers. I have seen a neurologist, gastrologist, hematologist, cardiologist, urologist, bone and joint specialist, and rheumatologist. Not one of these specialists could give me answers. We thought I was going to die. We felt hopeless. I was tired physically, mentally, emotionally, and spiritually.

I prayed and prayed for years, eleven years to be exact—eleven to twelve years of pain and frustration. My joints ached, and I had swelling in my left knee that caused me to be on crutches for two weeks. When I could not lift my arms to do my hair, I had to call one of my friends to go into her salon just to put my hair in a bun for my doctor's appointment. Jeesh! The memories. I also experienced headaches. I had stomach issues, I was feeling fatigued and dizzy at times, and I experienced numbness and tingling in my hands and feet;

I also had nerve pain in my spine. It was debilitating at times. It was disheartening. I got to the point where one day I found myself screaming in my SUV, sitting at a red light, "GOD, ARE YOU EVEN REAL?!" Yes, I was questioning the existence of God Almighty. I questioned it all. *Is God real? Is prayer real? What is prayer, anyway? Does God care about me? He, indeed, isn't responding to me.* I was angry, confused, weary, and hopeless. I felt abandoned by God.

One day, while praying and thinking about the Apostle Paul and the thorn in his side, I thought about the people who have lost their spouses or loved ones due to some type of illness. I told God if His plan for me was to transition to heaven, to let His will be done. I trusted Him to take care of my family. I decided God was sovereign, and if He was not going to heal me on this side of heaven, I was okay with it. Do I want that? No, but I have embraced that it could happen, and if it does, it is God's divine plan. I understand our days are numbered (Job 14:5). So I stopped allowing the enemy to torment me with those thoughts.

After casting that care on God, I continued to pray for healing. A year later, God spoke to me about my healing. He led me to many natural things to remedy my body and has caused me to overcome some of the issues I was experiencing. I have not experienced the fullness of my healing, but I am hoping for that breakthrough soon.

I wanted to share this with you so you can see how hard and long of a journey I have been on. The pressing, the persistence, and the waiting to receive the promise of God is not easy, and our faith is tried and tested. We also live in a fallen, broken world. One day, this will all pass away, though. In the meantime and between times, I encourage you to stay persistent. Keep serving, pressing, knocking, seeking, searching, and expecting. Keep making your request.

Wait A Minute, Q. Is God Real?

I cannot let you leave this chapter without addressing the question of the existence of God. I know there may be many individuals looking for the answer to this—one who may be seeking the truth to this question. So, here it is. Yes! God is indeed real. He does exist. Whether people want to believe it or not, He is real. I will show you in scripture.

"The heavens proclaim the glory of God, and the expanse proclaims the work of his hands" (Psalms 19:1).

Here is more. "Since what can be known about God is evident among them, because God has shown it to them. For his invisible attributes, that is, his eternal power and divine nature, have been clearly seen since the creation of the world, being understood through what he has made. As a result, people are without excuse" (Romans 1:19-20).

The scripture clearly says we can testify to God's existence through His creation. Many may not want to admit it, but there is no denying it. God exists. Even scripture tells us people will suppress the truth, and we see that happening today right before our eyes.

"For God's wrath is revealed from heaven against all godlessness and unrighteousness of people who by their unrighteousness suppress the truth" (Romans 1:18).

Many choose to suppress the truth because they want to live in lawlessness. They want what they want. They don't realize they are inviting the wrath of God into their lives. They do not realize that being friends with the world, loving the things of the world, is being an enemy of God. Lord have mercy!

Some individuals may speak of God but will not live to bring glory to His name with their lifestyles. They rather live the way they desire instead of fully submitting their lives and choices over to Him They want the benefit of knowing God without the sacrificial part. They rather not take up their cross to follow God. They will visit church occasinally, pray, even hold a coversation about God, but would rather keep participating in a lifestyle that is contrary to what they say they know and believe.

"For though they knew God, they did not glorify him as God or show gratitude. Instead, their thinking became worthless, and their senseless hearts were darkened" (Romans 1:21).

"They exchange the truth of God for a lie and worshiped and served what has been created instead of the Creator, who is praised forever. Amen" (Romans 1:25).

People have and will continue to deny the existence of God, as well as live the way they desire to live. To wrap up this chapter, let me reiterate I know God exists, my friends, even though I have questioned His existence in those frustrating, hard times.

"But for us, there is one God, the Father, by whom all things were created, and for whom we live. And there is one Lord, Jesus Christ, through whom all things were created, and through whom we live" (1 Corinthians 8:6, NLT).

Chapter 7
It's Not Just About You

Intercession—to intercede is to mediate or plead another's case for justice or mercy.

"Who is the one who condemns? Christ Jesus is the one who died, but even more, has been raised; he also is at the right hand of God and intercedes for us" (Romans 8:34).

"First of all, then, I urge that petitions, prayers, intercessions, and thanksgivings be made for everyone" (1 Timothy 2:1).

Intercession is another thing I remind my children to do regularly. Praying for others helps them understand the true meaning of being selfless and considerate. It also helps them to be more conscious of the many blessings they already have.

We should always be praying for others. Jesus does this for us, so why would we not do this for others? I remember praying with my adult son, my firstborn, who loves the Lord, a few years ago. As he listened to me, he shared how he became convicted. He explained how he heard me pray for others—strangers and situations in this world—and realized he wasn't doing that. He mentioned he would mainly cover his family and friends when praying and occasionally people experiencing homelessness. He called his prayer life shallow. Honestly, it was. Our hearts should break for everything God's heart breaks for and compel us to pray earnestly about those things.

Abraham was one of several in the Bible who made intercession for others. Abraham continued interceding for Sodom and Gomorrah, a city filled with wickedness. God listened to Abraham's continual requests, but sadly, God did not fulfill them because He could not even find ten righteous men (Genesis 18:16-33, 19:1-29). This biblical passage exemplifies how we should keep going to God for the lost and the broken until He releases us to stop praying for them.

It's tempting to give up on the individuals we pray for if it seems like nothing is changing, but we must continue to pray and keep the faith. Just because we don't see what God is doing behind the scenes in a person does not mean our prayers are not working. God may be working in that person the whole time. Remember that God desires that none shall perish but that all come to repentance (2 Peter 3:9).

Also, remember that when we pray for someone, we must never try to manipulate change in them. We have to be willing to let them go. We must hand them over to God. We shouldn't use scare tactics, threats,ven te,ars to get the person to change. These behaviors are unhealthy on so many levels. If you are struggling with this, ask God to help you let go and cover them in prayer.

I'd like to share a powerful story with you, but a funny one, too! I remember praying for my sister, who is a year apart from me. We are not just close in age but knit tight. When growing up, if you saw me, you saw her because we did everything together. We even dressed alike sometimes. People asked us if we were twins. Yeah, it was like that. So, when I gave my life to the Lord, I could not fathom the thought of my sister spending eternity in hell.

She did not know the Lord many years ago, but thank God she does now! Before she knew Christ and followed Him, she was living with her boyfriend, who is now her husband, and he is also a Christian now. HALLELUJAH! I prayed for her like crazy! I prayed she would know God as I knew Him. I prayed she would find no rest, peace, joy, or comfort in sin. Well, guess what? While I was praying, God was working. God was moving on my sister's heart with the very things I had asked Him to do. My sister had no peace till the point of her becoming restless. She had no idea what was happening to her. I had no idea God was causing this to occur in the heart of my sister, either. All of that fervent prayer for my sister was paying off.

A couple of years later, my sister had become so uncomfortable shacking up with her boyfriend she was willing to put him out. After talking to a lady at church and hearing that my sister's boyfriend would have nowhere to go, she advised her to let him stay and sleep on the sofa, but that was after talking to him about marriage and him being ready to marry.

By this time, they were both going to church. They lived together without sleeping together in the same bed or having sexual intercourse until they got married. Wow! All this happened in my sister's heart, and I had no idea she felt this way. I didn't learn this until years later, after she had given her life to God and shared this with me.

We now laugh because she asked me what I was praying for, and I told her. She responded, "I was suddenly wondering why I was so uncomfortable about my lifestyle." So now, we pray those same prayers for others and our families. My sister's testimony has taught us that prayer definitlty works behind the scenes.

I share this story to say we may never know what is going on in a person's heart or life when we pray for them. But God does. I think about the Apostle Paul as I write this. He was once named Saul and was persecuting Christians. He believed he was doing the right thing; it was not until Saul, now called Paul, had an encounter with Jesus, that his life changed. He went on to do great things for God, becoming one of the greatest missionaries the world has ever known.

The power of God can change hearts and minds. So, keep praying and standing in the gap for those who need it. The change you are waiting to see and experience may be right around the corner. Don't miss out on that victory.

So who should we be praying for? Our spouses, children, relatives, friends, co-workers, and the world. More specifically, we should pray for the church, our pastors and leaders in the church, and the body of Christ at large. We should pray for all nations. Pray for people in authority and serving our communities, like politicians, law enforcement, teachers, judges, and lawyers.

These individuals are making decisions that impact our lives and our children's lives. We need to pray for the right people who will practice good morals and make wise decisions as they put laws in place. We should pray to have the right officers upholding the law without corruption and racism. We should also pray that teachers take proper care of every student and that God graces every educator to fulfill their assignment.

We should also pray for our enemies. Some of you reading this may cringe at the idea, but it is vital. It not only keeps your heart from becoming stiff, bitter, and unforgiving but also changes you and may change the person you pray for. Jesus told us to pray for our enemies and to forgive. As stated before, praying for them does not mean you excuse or forget what they did to you. It does mean you forgive and release that person to God.

"Therefore, I tell you, her many sins have been forgiven; that's why she loved me so much. But the one who is forgiven little, loves little" (Luke 7:47). Can you say that you love God? Can you say you believe God loves you and forgives your sins? Do you see God as a hard taskmaster, a stern father, who keeps track of all your mistakes so that He can punish you for them? I did. I love God and desire to do His will, but I had a hard time believing He loves and forgives me.

This made it hard for me to forgive people who deeply hurt me because I did not believe or receive the forgiveness of God myself. It was hard to believe God no longer remembered my mistakes or sins, even knowing Hebrews 8:12 says, "For I will be merciful to their wrongdoing, and I will never remember their sins." I read this scripture like God only gave this forgiveness to the children of Israel. The enemy used this mindset of doubting God's forgiveness towards me to keep me in a state of unforgiveness.

Now that I have learned how to receive God's forgiveness freely, I am no longer holding people hostage for the sins they have committed against me. This is a hard pill to swallow when you feel like the person who wronged you does not deserve forgiveness, but God has forgiven us for our sins, so we must forgive others. Let me share this: in forgiving and praying for the people who wronged or will wrong us, we must ensure we do not permit toxic behavior because we are praying for individuals.

We may need to walk away from some relationships. I have had to do this with several individuals, but I continue praying for them. I pray God will allow them to see the error of their ways and allow Him to change their hearts. I pray God will heal them of any emotional trauma they may have experienced. I pray they will begin to see the hurt they are causing individuals.

I also pray they would take accountability for their actions and not blame others for their toxic behaviors. Finally, I continue to pray for my heart to be healed of the damage that the individuals caused and ask God to help me to always walk in love and kindness towards them and to speak well of them. These are just a few things I pray about regarding the people I had to walk away from.

To discover if you are in a toxic relationship, pray, asking God to show you if this person is unhealthy or just challenging at times. Another great idea is to talk to a therapist. Also, ask yourself, do I feel safe around this person? Do I have a voice around this person? Can I voice my opinion without this person attacking me? Am I always doing what they want and not what pleases me? Does this person act violently toward me? Are they physically hitting me? Are they emotionally abusing me, not allowing me to have feelings, or are they ever concerned about my feelings? Is this their normal behavior toward you—or anyone, for that matter?

Also, be sure you are not in a toxic relationship because you are toxic yourself. Make sure you are genuinely emotionally healthy. If you are not, seek help from a trusted counselor or therapist. You are valuable and deserve to be treated as such.

Another thing to consider is to meditate on scripture that says who you are in Christ. I use declarations every morning to replace the negative things the enemy tries to feed me about myself. Focus on scriptures like Psalm 139:14, which says, "I will praise you because I have been remarkably and wondrously made. Your works are wondrous, and I know this very well." Being in toxic relationships can most definitely cause us to view ourselves as worthless. It can also cause us to become toxic ourselves. We have all heard the saying, "Hurt people hurt people." For this reason, we should not allow ourselves to stay in toxic relationships.

Never allow anyone to make you think that staying in any toxic relationship is what God wants for you. I have allowed the wrong teaching of God's Word to keep me in toxic relationships for years. Ignorance on my part and theirs caused me years of unnecessary, deep hurt. Scriptures like, "Blessed are the peacemakers, for they will see God" (Matthew 5:9) do not mean we do not confront sin; it means the very opposite. We confront the person in their wrong, lovingly and peacefully, and try to resolve conflict. Being a peacemaker does not mean we tolerate abusive behavior.

"You are blessed when they insult you and persecute you and falsely say every kind of evil against you because of me" (Matthew 5:10). This verse talks about being persecuted because of Jesus and the gospel. So, the sister at your church can't use this to say your husband, who is coming home from work and taking his frustrations out on you by talking to you in an unloving and disrespectful way, is persecuting you for Christ. Not true! Foolishness. His behavior is toxic, unloving, and ungodly. Period! He needs some therapy to work through his anger issues. That's the truth.

A lot of the time, women who are giving this type of advice are emotionally unhealthy themselves and do not even realize they are. They mean well, but they are just ignorant of the scripture's context and their lack of emotional health. Do not get me wrong: in this situation, a woman should pray for her husband, love him, and be kind to him, but she should never believe her husband's behavior is acceptable. She should also never try to fix her husband's anger issues or make excuses for him. That is his job. He has to see his behavior is wrong, but he has to want to see it.

God never wants us to tolerate any form of abuse. There is nowhere in His Word from Genesis to Revelation where He condones or promotes abuse. We must study the Word of God ourselves and ensure we read it correctly, in its full context. That means we can not just pull out one verse and say it means something without reading the surrounding text. Doing this is dangerous and is why so many people have had to go through unnecessary hurt and disappointment.

I will leave you with this: pray for challenging people, but do not accept toxic behavior. We can pray and believe God will change people, but we are not the Savior, and people must want to change. God has given us all free will. He will never force us to do anything. God will nudge us. He will tug at our hearts but never force or control us. Knowing this truth is why I never promise a person their marriage will be restored. I know their marriage *can be* restored, but I don't know if it *will be*. I can pray and pray, but both people must be willing to open their hearts to God, emotional healing, and the possibility of restoration in their marriage. Now, pray, study, be wise, and be led by the Spirit of God.

Chapter 8
Why Even Pray?

So, why do we pray? We pray to communicate with God, confess our faults, and ask for forgiveness. We pray to give thanks to God. We pray to keep our hearts pure. We pray to intercede for others. We pray to get instruction, direction, and answers from God. We ultimately pray God's will be done.

Praying for a pure heart

Praying for a pure heart is one of the things we must always do. I do this daily for myself as well as for the people I am praying for. Jeremiah 17:9 mentions how the heart is deceitful above all things, which is why I constantly run to Jesus about my own heart. Everything we do and say flows from our hearts.

"A good person produces good out of the good stored in his heart. An evil person produces evil out of the evil stored up in his heart, for his mouth speaks from the overflow of his heart" (Luke 6:45).

What we do and say speaks a lot about what we have going on in our hearts. We must listen carefully to what we are saying and to what others are saying, especially if they are repeatedly saying it. Sometimes, a person may say something and quickly say they didn't mean what they said, but how often are they saying it? This person's words signify what's happening in their heart. We ought not to disregard what people say repetitively. It may be protecting us from danger and heartache. Pay attention to the signs! The signs don't lie.

Many, many years ago, when I was about twenty, I was walking to my car with an old friend from a party. This guy approached me and asked me if he could have my number. Cell phones were somewhat non-existent back then. Whew! Thank God! The reason for my relief was because this guy was very persistent. He was downright annoying. He grabbed me by my wrist and said he would not let go until I agreed to give him my phone number. As I looked over at my friend, who was upset, asking him to release my wrist, my brilliant mind concocted a plan. I told him I would give him my number. So, I gave him the digits, but I gave him an old phone number to one of my other friends. After handing him the paper, this guy had the audacity to ask me to repeat the number. I knew it because it was my friend's old number and I called it out to him. He nodded while smiling and said he would call me the next day. So he thought.

Even if I'd found him highly attractive, I would have never given him my number. Why? Because of the signs. He was too aggressive—meaning he probably was controlling, overly jealous, and abusive. His behavior said a lot about what was in his heart. It always does. So pay close attention to others' words and actions and your own. Keep your heart pure through prayer, humility, transparency, and growing closer and closer to God. There is no other way.

Instruction and Direction

"Trust in the Lord with all your heart, and do not rely on your own understanding; in all your ways acknowledge him, and he will make your path straight" (Proverbs 3:5-6).

Asking God for instruction and direction is so important. We can make some pretty messed up choices without seeking God. I have made some myself. Many individuals never seek God in prayer about their decisions. The Word of God tells us, "A person's steps are established by the Lord, and he takes pleasure in his way" (Psalms 37:23).

If we allow God to have His way in our lives, then we can trust He will guide us if we let Him. Sometimes, this means we will get what we want. But I am so grateful God didn't always allow me to have what I asked for and that I allowed Him to guide me. Sometimes, it is hard to figure out what is best for us. It is also challenging to believe God has a better plan for us, especially when we think what we ask Him for is good for us. We can't see the whole picture. God knows the whats and why's about our situations. It is tempting to draw our own conclusion when we strongly desire something. Patience and trust are the keys, though. We have to be patient while praying and trust God will guide us on the best path.

I remember praying to God many years ago and asking Him to restore my previous marriage. I thank God He did not give me what I asked for but instructed me to let go of that unhealthy marriage. I would have been miserable because we were on two different life paths. I wanted a personal relationship with the Lord, but he did not. He desired to keep living unholy and unfaithful. At first it was hard to think of life without my ex-husband. It was not easy to let go, especially after spending a whole year praying for God to restore the marriage. But as I pondered on how detrimental and wrong my marital situation was, I began to see how letting go was the best choice for me and my son. I thank God for giving me the strength and grace to let go. I am thankful for knowing His will and acting on it. I have no regrets.

Although God desired the previous marriage to work, He will never force a person to change. He gives us all free will. But because of God's loving nature, He permitted me to leave that toxic marriage. Two years later, I met my current husband, the man who loves and serves God with me, the man who understands real *agape* love, maturity, and marriage.

My willingness to trust God and let go of that failed relationship allowed me to receive my blessing. I had no idea what God had in store for me, but I am so glad I allowed Him to lead me. Even when it seemed like I was losing in the beginning by letting go of that bad marriage and raising my son as a single mother, I chose to walk away. Well, I can say this: God used that relationship to bless me with my amazing son and used that marriage to grow my prayer life. I am grateful for those things. Now, had I held on to that marriage for whatever reason, it would have kept me in bondage and years of unhappiness and toxicity. Lord, THANK YOU! Today, I implore you to trust God's plan and path for your life. It is so worth it.

We Have Divine Guidance Through the Holy Spirit

We can see throughout the Bible where God gave His people instructions. He instructed Adam, Noah, Moses, and the Israelites. We, too, have the Word, the Spirit of God, to guide and direct us in our choices. All we have to do is ask for direction, and God will give it to us.

Second Peter 1:3 states, "His divine power has given us everything required for life and godliness through the knowledge of him who called us by his own glory and goodness." Yes, God has given us everything we need as it pertains to our lives because we walk in the knowledge of Him, and with that knowledge comes divine guidance.

This knowledge instructs us in our conduct and decision-making. This knowledge leads us in our relationships with our spouses, children, family, and friends. This knowledge guides us on our jobs and the road. The knowledge of God directs us in all areas of life if we simply allow it to. I have talked with many individuals who do not want their steps ordered by God. They do not wish to have His divine guidance. My heart aches for those people because they miss experiencing the many blessings they can receive by allowing God to order their steps.

The Great Yes

Think of Mary, the mother of Jesus. The angel of the Lord appeared to her and said the Holy Spirit would impregnate her with the world's Savior. God even instructed her on what to name the child and the direction she and Joseph were going. What God was asking her to do seemed impossible, and I am sure she was afraid and confused, but she decided to trust the plan of God for her life and said yes. She knew God would not fail at His divine purpose.

Wow, God trusted Mary to take care of Jesus well.

If you are a stay-at-home mom, be proud of your assignment. Be proud of your ministry. Be proud—not prideful but proud—to serve your family. Never let anyone put you down or make you feel less than for doing what God has called you to do. Understanding what God has instructed you to do is not everyone's business. You don't have to feel the weight of explaining your life to people.

I had my share of wanting people to see, know, and respect my ministry of being a stay-at-home mom and the purpose for this season of my life for years. God has entrusted you to care for your household well. He trusts you to rear your children well. I had to come to this conclusion for myself. Gosh, it took me years to grasp this. I cried, fussed, and was frustrated because I had to be home caring for my family while watching my friends go and get it. Whatever IT means. We sometimes compare our lives to others and miss what God has given us to enjoy.

Sometimes, the thing God asks us to do may be challenging. Many times, it is. Sometimes, what God is instructing us to do may not make sense to us. As stated earlier, it is all about faith—the belief God has a perfect plan. God does have the perfect plan for our lives. All we have to do is move when He tells us to move, go where He is telling us to go, stay when He is telling us to stay, and do what He calls us to do. Mary, Joseph, and many others in the Bible did it.

I will not ask what would have happened to the world if Mary had not said yes to God. I would be placing limitations on Him. I am sure God could have chosen someone else to do it, but Mary would have missed out on such a divine opportunity that was such a massive blessing for herself and those involved. This divine opportunity was her assignment, her purpose—the thing that brings us the most fulfillment. Our divine purpose can only be discovered when we permit God to instruct us. Pause and meditate on that for a while. Your divine purpose is found by listening and obeying the instructions of God. There is no other way, my friend.

Chapter 9
It's All about Humility

"Whenever you pray, you must not be like the hypocrites because they love to pray, standing in the synagogue and street corners to be seen by people. Truly, I tell you, they have their reward. But when you pray, go into your private room, shut the door, and pray to your Father who is in secret. And your Father who sees you in secret will reward you. When you pray, don't babble like the Gentiles, since they imagine they'll be heard for their many words. Don't be like them because your Father knows the things you need before you ask" (Matthew 6:5-8).

This scripture is critical for our prayer lives and our lives in general. We must remain humble. We should not be proud and arrogant people. This type of behavior only happens when we leave our insecurities unchecked. We become prideful. Full of ugly, stinky pride. YUCK! Pride stinks in the nostrils of people, but most of all, in the nostrils of God. The Word says God resists the proud but gives grace to the humble (James 4:6). Humility is always the answer. Stay humble in all things. We do not have to prove ourselves to anyone or put on a show.

Trust me—trying to prove yourself to people constantly putting you down and making accusations against you can be challenging. Those people treating you like this know they have insecurities and do not like themselves, so for that reason, they are accusing you and putting you down. Hand these people over to God and pray for them continually. Let them do what they do. We must learn how to let people own their brokenness. Don't let people's opinions, accusations, lies, or even their rejection cause you to see yourself as invaluable. Your worth is not in what they think of you. Don't let yourself slip into pride by trying to prove something to them or defend yourself. It is so not worth it.

Remember, God knows you and sees you. Just stay connected to Him. We are living primarily for an audience of one, God. Our goal is always to please Him, not man. If our lives are pleasing to God, we can be sure we are living and relating to people the way we should. So, stop focusing on the naysayers and keep your eyes on God and His purpose for your life. Let God exalt and vindicate you. Make sure you are emotionally healthy. When we are not emotionally healthy, we have this disposition to gain people's approval. Love yourself, embrace yourself, and let people's opinions of you go. We are all entitled to our opinions, but our views are not always one-size-fits-all. Stop trying to prove yourself.

People will see all God is doing in our lives when we stay connected to Him and walk humbly. Deep, genuine intimacy with God will help us continually operate in a spirit of humility. Even when the enemy tries to tempt us to fall into pride, spending daily time with the Lord will expose the spirit of pride that may try to rear its ugly head. God will see our desire for humility as we persistently seek Him, and people will see our deep connection to God through our lifestyle.

Think about this. When a loving husband and wife share sexual intimacy, it causes them to grow closer. No one can see the intimacy they share or their sexual connection; no one can see the oxytocin release, but people can tell they enjoy one another by the way they relate to one another in public. People can tell by their body language (posture) and words (praise of one another).

The way people can see the closeness of that husband and wife is the same way people can see our proximity to God. Just as I can carry the scent of my husband's cologne on me just by holding him, we can become so close to God we begin to smell like the sweet aroma He carries after being in His presence. Just as the length of my marriage has caused me and my husband to develop some of each other's habits, we can be so close to God we begin to look and act like Him.

How we act and what we say about God speaks volumes about our relationship with Him. Once again, never pray or do anything to be seen or heard by people. Doing this for that reason will cause us to lose out on the blessings of God and ultimately bring us embarrassment. We will be humbled in some way and at some point.

Two words come to mind that can be found in the word *pride: I* and *die. I* is a word or letter wrapped up in pride: I want to be seen, I want to be heard, I want to be celebrated, I want to be served. I, I, and I is what the prideful person is all about. They rarely think about the other person. They are too focused on what makes them happy or comfortable. Some would even step on others to get what they think they deserve. It doesn't matter how they hurt the other person involved. The prideful person just wants what they want. In many cases, they believe they deserve it. The prideful person believes they are not wrong about their actions. Don't get me wrong, we all have prideful moments. Being prideful is not the way we should live, though.

This type of pride was the case for Satan; a case of the I's got him in trouble. Satan was once a beautiful angelic being, but he rebelled against God because of pride.

"You said to yourself, 'I will ascend to the heavens. I will set up my throne above the stars of God. I will sit on the mount of God's assembly, in the remotest parts of the North. I will ascend above the highest clouds; I will make myself like the Most High" (Isaiah 14:13-14).

We must be careful not to become like Satan. We must ensure we are not after God's glory but seeking to bring all the glory to Him. Once again, our unchecked insecurities cause us to look to be exalted. Don't get me wrong—I am not saying we should not allow people to compliment or celebrate us. To keep it simple and help us keep pride away, ask yourself, "What is my motive for wanting this? How do I feel when I don't get continual praise or validation? Am I angry and all bent out of shape?" Be honest about where you are. Honesty is the key to genuine growth and change.

Next, I want to touch on the word *die*. We want to die to ourselves daily, as Paul says in 1 Corinthians 15:31: "I face death every day, as surely as I may boast about you, brothers and sisters, in Christ Jesus our Lord." When we don't fail to die to ourselves, our beliefs, and our desires, we leave room for our flesh and pride to come in and take over.

We should always look to die to our desires and embrace God's desires. Keep in mind the enemy doesn't want you to die to your flesh, but he does want you to die. Remember, his nature is to kill, steal, and destroy. He will lie to us to get us to do things that will bring death to our lives. Once you choose the path of death, then bam! That joker has done his job and left you there in your mess. All because you didn't choose to die to your flesh. Don't let the enemy win because of pride. Choose humility; choose life. There can be no real breakthrough or change without true alignment of your heart toward God. Humble yourself before God, my friend. Let Him work on you, in you, and through you. All for His glory.

Chapter 10
It's Time To Pray

Before we dive into prayer, let me say this: prayer should not be about rules, rituals, or traditions. We can pray anywhere and from any posture, as long as the heart posture is correct. We can stand, kneel, and walk when we pray. We can also pray while we lie down in our beds (I can't do this too often, though. I will fall asleep!). We can also pray in our car, in the shower, at our desk—you name it. We can pray just about anywhere we feel led to pray.

Although we can pray just about anywhere, we need to set aside some quiet time to pray to hear God without distractions. Don't be afraid to pray. It is not as complicated as some people make it out to be. It is about you and your relationship with the Lord, not what someone else does or says. It's about the posture of your heart, not necessarily about the eloquent words you use or how long you pray.

I have seen and known many individuals who can pray well and even know scripture references, but their hearts are far from God. They pray His Word but refuse to let God into their hearts. They would rather live life the way they want instead of fully submitting to the ways of the Lord. This type of heart posture is dangerous. It also raises the question of how they can be so content with their failure to walk in the way of the Lord. It raises the question of their salvation. Are they saved? Did they repent? Did they allow God to place His Holy Spirit in them? Because their actions show otherwise. For example, I know individuals who say they know God and claim to be saved but they habitually commit sexual acts with their boyfriends or girlfriends. Some have been living with them for years, and when the question of marriage came up, they became angry. They even accused me and other individuals of being judgemental. They didn't understand that to love them is to hold them accountable. To love them is to challenge them to do better. Would I do this for an individual who never confessed to having a relationship with the Lord? No, because unbelievers practice sin. They have not been made new through the power of the Holy Spirit. The conversation with an unbeliever would be about Jesus, how He saved and delivered me, and how He could do the same thing for them.

Matthew 7:22-23, "On that day many will say to me, 'Lord, Lord, didn't we prophesy in your name, drive out demons in your name, and do many miracles in your name?' Then I will announce to them, 'I never knew you. Depart from me, you lawbreakers!'" We don't always know who has a genuine relationship with Jesus Christ, and it is not our job to try and figure that part out. We live according to the Word and let our light shine in the darkness. We allow people to live out their lives as we pray for them when we see habitual sinful behaviors. It is all on them if they live religiously and pretend to know God. We all have free will. We all have a choice to live how we desire.

I am not saying we should not judge. People are quick to throw that saying out there. You know, the Tupac Shakur song, "Only God Can Judge Me." I firmly believe this phrase is used by individuals who practice sin and want a pass for it. Do they not know the Bible states we can judge? Let's look at it. "Do not judge, so that you won't be judged. For you will be judged by the same standard with which you judge others, and you will be measured by the same measure you use. Why do you look at the splinter in your brother's eye but don't notice the beam of wood in your own eye? Or how can you say to your brother, 'Let me take the splinter out of your eye,' and look, there's a beam of wood in your own eye? Hypocrites! First take the beam of wood out of your eye, and then you will see clearly to take the splinter out of your brother's eye. Don't give what is holy to the dogs or toss your pearls before pigs, or they will trample them under their feet, turn, and tear you to pieces" (Matthew 7:1-6).

People misuse this scripture. This scripture is not saying we should not judge but that we should judge through the lense of the Holy Spirit. We should use the Word of God, the only standard we live by as Christians, to judge individuals and situations. We should ensure we live holy lifestyles before judging others for their sins. We should not be hypocrites. We must also be mindful of who we try to share the gospel with. Those who practice religion and live sinful lifestyles will oppose the Word and oppose you for it. In Matthew 7:16-20, the text says, "You'll recognize them by their fruit. Are grapes gathered from thornbushes or figs from thistles? In the same way, every good tree produces good fruit, but every bad tree produces bad fruit. A good tree can't produce bad fruit; neither can a bad tree produce good fruit. Every tree that doesn't produce good fruit is cut down and thrown into the fire. So you'll recognize them by their fruit."

Going back to prayer, we should never have to compete or compare ourselves to anyone else, even if someone can pray very well or we find them very articulate. They may not even know God. They may know of Him but not intimately. We should never compare ourselves because this is unhealthy. Comparing ourselves may show there is some type of insecurity issue. Comparison is also the breeding ground for the spirit of jealousy to enter our hearts.

Sadly, I have been guilty of this comparison and jealousy issue. Guess what? One of those times was against my own husband. Lord, Jesus. Hold on, let me explain. Not to justify but to clarify, share the whole story, and share the root cause. Many years ago, I decided to get my degree in psychology. My husband and I felt God calling us to counsel couples. It was evident. We met with couples, and I was always ministering to women about their marriages and relationships. I started at a community college with plans to transfer after completing my two-year degree. I had it all planned out. My two younger daughters had started pre-k and kindergarten, and now it was time for me to go after my goals. It was time for me to become a career woman.

During my third semester, I started to experience heart palpitations as I walked across campus. Then, along with those palpitations, I developed constant headaches. I had no clue what was going on. I scheduled a doctor's appointment, and all I got was a referral to a neurologist who gave me a prescription for depression medication, which I trashed after taking the first one. Why? Because I wasn't clinically depressed. Wow! Crazy, right? Since I had no answers, I finished that semester and decided to schedule my classes for the following semester. About a week later, I felt like the Holy Spirit was leading me to drop those classes. What! *This has got to be the devil,* I thought. I continued to feel that nudge. *Drop the classes.* So, finally, I did. I dropped the classes and cried like a baby.

A few weeks after dropping those classes, I continued to get sicker and sicker. I had no clue why. After days of crying and being disappointed about my setback, I was relieved I hadn't started that semester and failed because of my health issue. I said to myself, "After this is over, I'll just go back and finish school." Failing that semester would have upset me because I was a huge perfectionist. Thank God I have gotten better over the years. Nearing the end of my second semester, my husband also decided to start online school to get his degree in psychology.

Well. Unbeknownst to me, I would have to quit school and watch my husband achieve the very thing I decided to go after myself. I became jealous of my own husband. Yuck! Shame on me, right? I felt like God was overlooking me and allowing my husband to achieve what I believed He should have allowed me to achieve. After all, it was my idea first; I was the one praying and reading my Bible more. I was the one who was always trying to please God by obeying Him and walking in love. It was me, me, me. My comparison caused me to become jealous because I believed I was better than my husband. I believed I was more spiritual and considerate of others, so God should have allowed me to get the degree. I saw my husband's stinky, ugly arrogance, selfishness, and pride but didn't recognize mine. Well, not until the Holy Spirit quickly showed me. I had the case of the I's. Lord! I had to repent to the Lord, and I went to my husband, who had no clue I felt this way. I apologized and told him I was proud of what he had accomplished. And honestly, I was. I just let the insecurity of feeling like a nobody with no degree, career, or job get in the way of celebrating him.

I also compared myself to many successful and working women I know. I was "just" a stay-at-home mother who was sick with an illness no one could figure out. I was a liability. I was bringing more harm than good to my marriage. I was adding pressure and struggle. And the things my husband had said to me in the past in his arrogance and ignorance during our arguments, things like, "We are not compatible" and "You're not suitable for me," had so much weight and volume to them now.

That, coupled with my own need for healing from my past of abuse and rejection, caused me to feel like I had no worth. The trauma that caused that mindset of performance-based love and reward had arisen. I felt that if I was doing well, performing well, and seeking God passionately, He should have allowed me to pursue what I was going after; after all, it was a good thing. Aren't credentials respected in society? I would have used it to help people. I would have used it to glorify Him. These lies and feelings of insecurity caused the enemy to plant a seed of jealousy in my heart. I prayed daily and asked God to heal me and keep jealousy out of my heart.

We must ensure we do not allow the enemy to come in and plant seeds of jealousy. We don't want to become like Saul, who God appointed as king of the Israelites. Saul, who was jealous of David to the point of wanting and trying to kill him. Saul was fine with killing his thousand men until David began receiving praise for killing ten thousand. Saul allowed his insecurities to cause him to compare himself to David, and jealousy arose (1 Samuel 18). Saul had become so jealous of David's success he grew full of hate towards him.

But Saul did not realize David was successful in all he did because the Lord's hand was upon him. Saul was not humble enough to recognize we can do nothing ourselves; it is the power of God and the divine will of God to use us the way He chooses to use us. Knowing this truth will always help us keep things in perspective when the enemy tries to plant seeds of jealousy with our insecurities. Does God want to use us in the capacity He is using the individual we are comparing ourselves to? Can God trust us to steward that type of assignment well? Is that what God called us to do? We must acknowledge and deal with our insecurities so they do not overtake us.

The Bible shows Saul already had insecurities before David showed up on the scene. He considered himself "less than" as he spoke to the prophet Samuel. Here is what the text says: "Saul responded, 'Am I not a Benjaminite from the smallest of Israel's tribes and isn't my clan the least important of all the clans of the Benjaminite tribe? So why have you said something like this to me?'" (1 Samuel 9:21).

Listen, the enemy will always offer suggestions, but we must keep him from planting seeds on the grounds of our hearts. Yes, we tend to think about our minds and thoughts but neglect to address the matter of our hearts. I encourage you to read Luke 8 on the parable of the sower. Jesus is talking about the ground of our hearts. We must care for and guard the ground of our hearts. Pray when you sense the spirit of jealousy and comparison entering your mind. Pray immediately. Seek to find the root cause of the feeling of jealousy. If you need therapy to overcome those feelings, then get it.

By the way, my husband got his associate's degree in psychology and Christian counseling but could not achieve his bachelor's degree or go any further. He only needed two more classes to finish his bachelor's degree, but I got sicker, and he couldn't handle the pressure of school, working full time, watching me suffer with no answers, and all the financial hardships we were facing, so he quit, too. We both have not gotten to the finish line with school and have not had the money or time to go back. We don't stress about it, though. We know God can do things the way He desires to do them. It may not be the way we planned. It may be something far more significant or unimaginable. His timing is always perfect, and character preparation is vital.

Please remember we should celebrate others' gifts and accomplishments but never be jealous or covetous. It is okay for us to see someone passionate about what they do or successful in something, and allow it to push us, spark a fire, and challenge us to do more, but we should not become envious or want to be them. We were created to become exactly who God created us to become and do what He created us to do. Stay in your lane. Be your authentic self, flaws and all. You are a beautiful mess, a masterpiece.

Now, start talking to God as if you are talking to a natural person in the room. It's really that simple. You can also pray scripture. Praying scripture is something I love doing. Both ways are good, but I always think about how Jesus spoke the scripture when the devil tried to tempt Him. IT IS WRITTEN, devil! You can read about this in the book of Matthew 4:1-11.

Spiritual Warfare

We cannot talk about prayer without discussing spiritual warfare. As believers of the gospel, we will undoubtedly encounter spiritual warfare. There is no way around it. Why? Because we have an enemy who hates us and the God we serve. Jesus told Simon the enemy was after him. "Simon, Simon, look out. Satan has asked to sift you as wheat" (Luke 22:31). Doesn't this remind you of Job? Satan was looking to get after Job. Satan is always looking to attack us, too.

First Peter 5:8 says, "Be sober-minded, be alert. Your adversary, the devil, is prowling around like a roaring lion, looking for anyone he can devour." Some people don't believe the devil exists. They think he is some made-up character they see in movies or cartoons. You know, the one sitting on the person's shoulder in the red suit with horns and a tail, holding a pitchfork while whispering in the person's ear. They think it's all fun and games; it's all make-believe. They don't have a clue how real the demonic is. They don't realize there is a spiritual realm we can't see with the naked eye. They don't understand there is such a thing called spiritual warfare. We have to know the truth so we can have victory.

The Apostle Paul tells the church of Ephesus about spiritual warfare in chapter 6 of the book of Ephesians. "Finally, be strengthened in the Lord and his vast strength. Put on the full armor of God so that you can stand against the schemes of the devil. For our struggle is not against flesh and blood, but against the rulers, against the authorities, against the cosmic powers of this darkness, against evil, spiritual forces in the heavens" (Ephesians 6:10-12).

Paul told the Ephesian church what they were up against and gave them the solution. He told them that because they were up against these things, they needed to take up the whole armor of God to resist the evil they would face and gain victory.

"For this reason, take up the full armor of God, so that you may be able to resist the evil day, and having prepared everything, to take your stand. Stand, therefore, with truth like a belt around your waist, righteousness like armor on your chests, and your feet sandaled with readiness for the gospel of peace. In every situation take up the shield of faith with which you can extinguish all the flaming arrows of the evil one. Take the helmet of salvation and the sword of the Spirit—which is the word of God" (Ephesians 6:13-17).

I don't know about you, but when I see the word *belt*, I think about how it holds up a pair of pants. The scripture says we should wear the belt of truth around our waist, so we should allow the truth to hold us up instead of crumbling. Do you know the truth? Do you know the truth about God, His Word, your situation, and yourself? These are essential questions, but most importantly, do you have the correct answers? For us to stand in truth, we have to know it. Do you know the truth?

It then mentions wearing the breastplate of righteousness and the feet being sandaled with the gospel of peace. The breastplate protects our hearts from becoming hard toward God when the enemy comes in with lies and accusations. Instead of believing those lies and accusations, we believe the truth of God's Word because we have guarded our hearts with the breastplate of righteousness.

Instead of allowing those fiery darts to take us out by bombarding our minds, we are sandaled in the gospel of peace. We are standing in the peace of God. We are walking in the peace of God. We know we walk by faith. We live by faith. We take up our shield of faith when the weapons are fiercely coming at us. We hide behind the Word of God. We hide in the blood covering of Jesus Christ. We allow the helmet of salvation to protect our minds when the enemy tells us the battle is too complicated or life is too hard.

We must know we are never fighting for victory but from a place of victory. The battle belongs to our God. He has already won it for us. All we must do is take the sword of the Spirit, the Word of God, and use it on our enemy, the devil. How do we do that? We do precisely what the Apostle Paul told the church of Ephesus to do. We pray. We stay alert. We persevere. We intercede. Why do we intercede? Because our fellow sisters and brothers in Christ need our prayers. They are in a battle, too. Praying for others helps us take the focus off ourselves, builds us, and helps us persevere. Like real combat soldiers, we realize we are not just fighting the battle for ourselves but for the one next to us. So, we intercede for them, too. Also, when we win and share our testimonies, God is glorified by our victory, but our sisters and brothers in Christ are no longer horrified. They see God can do great things and are encouraged and strengthened to stand and fight in prayer.

This fight is hard, but we must continue fighting the good fight of faith, my friend. We have to stay in the race. That is what it says in 2 Timothy 4:7. We are soldiers in God's army. Let us remember that. But remember, we cannot do it in our strength, either. When you find yourself doing this, be reminded of Zechariah 4:6, which says, "Not by might, nor by power, but by My Spirit, says the Lord of Hosts."

We can do nothing apart from God. Only by the Spirit of the Living God can we accomplish anything. Remember this truth when you are tempted to give up on prayer and are still waiting for those prayers to manifest, my friend.

Remember that the enemy is always trying to keep you from receiving what you ask God for or are asking Him to do. Think about Daniel. What happened when he prayed? A figure who is referred to as the prince of the kingdom of Persia opposes the angel who was assigned to Daniel. Just as Daniel prayed and experienced demonic pushback, we will have demonic forces that try to keep our prayers from being carried out. The text mentions Daniel's prayers were heard, though. What stood out to me the most when I read this verse is how heaven heard Daniel's prayers from the first day he purposed to understand and humble himself before God.

"'Don't be afraid, Daniel,' he said to me, 'for from the first day that you purposed to understand and humble yourself before your God, your prayers were heard. I have come because of your prayers'" (Daniel 10:12).

So let me ask: Is your heart purposed to understand and humble yourself before God? If not, maybe this is why you haven't seen a breakthrough. I am examining myself, too, my friend. Are we really trying to gather understanding when we pray? Are we operating in humility when we pray? Lord, please show us if we aren't doing these things. We want our prayers to be heard in heaven and answered by God. We want you to send Your ministering angels to perform Your will and promises in our lives.

Returning to the text about Daniel, it mentions the angel on assignment for Daniel was opposed for twenty-one days. This twenty-one-day opposition made him call for some holy backup. Michael, the archangel, came to help get things done. Micheal or Mikael, whose Hebrew meaning is "Who is like God," an angel, showed up on the scene for Daniel. Just as Micheal showed up for Daniel, God will ensure we always have a heavenly, holy host to fight on our behalf.

So, when we pray, we must know and believe God is working on our behalf. Don't let the enemy's threats silence you. Isn't it amazing how Daniel did not allow the king's decree to keep him from praying to God, even though he knew he would be thrown in the lions' den? Ohh Lord! Some of us may very well have to think hard about that. Nah, Lord, I don't know if I am ready for the lion's den. Daniel was a courageous man.

Just as Daniel continued in prayer, we must not allow the enemy to use the challenging times we face to stop us from praying. Giving up on prayer can sometimes become very tempting, but we must keep asking, seeking, and knocking until the door opens. The enemy will never just hand over anything to us. We must fight to get it and fight to keep it. He is not just going to allow you to have a great marriage. He wants to keep you from starting that business. He wants to keep you from walking in your purpose. The enemy will not allow you to do anything that would benefit you or others. He will always come up against us. Yep, we have to fight, fight, and keep on fighting. It's all good, though, because if God is for us, who can be against us?

Let Me Leave You With This

I cannot promise God will answer every prayer you bring before Him the way you desire Him to. I would be giving you false hope. Some things we experience will leave us wondering why God allowed them to happen the way they did. Some things we experience might cut us so deep and make us feel like someone has knocked the life out of us! We will all experience some form of trauma, hurt, disappointment, struggle, loss, or hardship.

These things will certainly make us feel like God has forgotten, rejected, or abandoned us. That is the truth. So, while I can not promise you a life free of pain, I can promise you that you are important to God, and He cares about and loves you. How can I say this? Because His Word says so, and as much as the traumas of my life cause me to struggle to believe He loves me, I believe His Word. I believe He exists, and I believe He is who He says He is. Why? Because I have seen His goodness in my life and the lives of others.

I can see it in all of the chaos around me. I can see it through His creation; I can feel it through His peace He gives me as I am going through physical pain in my body, as I am going through financial difficulties, and as I wait to see where my future is heading. God is real, indeed! I encourage you to keep going to Him in prayer. Keep seeking His face. He loves you.

You are valuable to Him even if people have made you feel you are not. I know this has been an issue for me over the years, but I am learning to see the value in myself and know I have many great qualities God has blessed me with.

I have learned that people who do not value me have no business being part of my life, and I am okay with that. Listen, God wants to show up for you, even if people have let you down. God cares about everything we face, our issues, the storms of life, and all the twists and turns that life throws at us. God is in it all. He is for us. Remember, the Son of God was with Daniel in the lion's den. The Son of God was with Shadrach, Meshach, and Abednego(Daniel 3:24-30) in the fiery furnace, and the Son of God is always with us in our trials.

So, when you feel abandoned by God, I want to encourage you to look again. When those prayers are seemingly not answered, look again. When you feel like nothing is happening, look again. When you feel frustrated, look again, my friend. Just as the servant of Elijah, who looked seven times for rain, we must keep looking for God to move in our lives (1 Kings 18:42-45). The servant didn't see anything those six times he looked, but that seventh time, he experienced what he had been going back and forth to see. Don't give up on prayer, and don't give up on God. Look again. God is there in it all. God is real, and so are His promises for your life. Whatever He promises us, He will fulfill. You can definitely believe that. So keep praying until you see a breakthrough.

Even if that is healing from a broken heart, the loss of a loved one, a divorce, a miscarriage, financial difficulties, health issues, or rejection. Keep going to God. Keep looking for Him to show up for you with strength, encouragement, support, healing, joy, peace, and the grace to keep moving forward. Just take it one day at a time, my friend. God is right there with you. He is in it all. He is real!

Prayer For Your Insecurities

Father God, I come to you in the Mighty name of Jesus, the name above every name, The name above every ill-spoken word, every accusation, every lie, and every insecurity in my life. Father, I thank You that I don't allow people's opinions, perceptions, and perspectives about me and their rejection of me cause me to view myself as invaluable. I praise You because my worth and identity are found in Jesus Christ! Lord, thank You for being the God of my salvation and adopting me into Your sonship. Father, You have chosen me. You love me, and nothing can separate me from Your love. Father, I thank You for setting Your stamp of approval on me. You have called me out of darkness and into Your marvelous light. I am remarkably and wonderfully made by You. I am the apple of Your eye and worth more than many sparrows. I thank You, Father God, for making me in Your image and after Your likeness. I am the righteousness of God in Christ Jesus, and I have put on the new self, the one created in righteousness in purity of the truth. I am a new creation in Christ; old things have passed away, and the new has come. I thank You, God, that I am no longer a slave to my sinful nature but have become a slave to righteousness. Father, I thank You that I am heard by You, I am seen by You, and I am known by You. You are always with me. You care for me. In Jesus' name, Amen!

Scripture References

Habakkuk 3:18, Ephesians 1:5 & 1:11, 1 John 4:15, Romans 8:38-39, 2 Timothy 2:19, 1 Peter 2:9, Psalm 139:13-14, Psalm 17:8, Matthew 10:31, Genesis 1:26, 2 Corinthians 5:21, Ephesians 4:24, 2 Corinthians 5:17, Romans 6:18, 1 John 5:14, 1 Peter 3:12, Psalm 139:1-4 Matthew 28:20, 1 Peter 5:7

Prayer For Purity

Lord, help me to continue to walk by the Spirit so I would not carry out the desire of the flesh. Keep me from sexual immorality, moral impurity, promiscuity, idolatry, sorcery, hatred, strife, jealousy, outbursts of anger, selfish ambitions, dissension, factions, envy, drunkenness, carousing, and anything similar, because I know those who practice such things will not inherit the kingdom of God. Lord, I thank You that I belong to You; because I belong to You, I have crucified the flesh with its passions and desires. I have put to death what belongs to my earthly nature: sexual immorality, impurity, lust, evil desires, and greed, which is idolatry. Father, help me to always walk in love, joy, peace, kindness, goodness, faithfulness, and self-control. I recognize that in Christ, I am a new creation; the old has passed away, and the new has come. In Jesus' name, I pray, Amen!

Scripture References
    Galatians 5:16, Galatians 5:19-21, Colossians 3:5, Galatians 5:22-23, 2 Corinthians 5:17

A Prayer For Anger Issues

Father, I come to You in the name of Jesus. I ask that You would uproot and do away with the spirit of anger in my life. Help me to be quick to listen, slow to speak, and slow to anger because human anger does not accomplish God's righteousness. Help me to put away anger, wrath, malice, slander, and filthy language from my mouth. Spirit of the Living God, help me never to allow my spirit to rush into anger because anger abides in the heart of fools. Instead, help me to refrain from anger and give up rage. I understand it can only bring harm. An angry person stirs up conflict, and a hot-tempered one increases rebellion. So, Father God, keep me from acting like the fool who gives full vent to his anger. Father, help me to be the righteous person who keeps their anger in check. In Jesus' name, I pray, Amen!

Scripture References

James 1:19-20, Colossians 3:8, Ecclesiastes 7:9, Psalm 37:8, Proverbs 29:22, Proverbs 29:11

A Prayer Against Fear

Father, I come to You today declaring Your word against the spirit of fear in my life. I know You have not given me the spirit of fear but power, love, and a sound mind. So, I declare I am not afraid of anything or anyone. I know fear torments and Your perfect love casts out fear. So, Father, I thank You that I operate in Your perfect love. Your Word says to fear not, so I am standing on Your Word today. I declare that fear will not paralyze me or hold me hostage. I am not afraid of anyone because You will be with me to deliver me. I know the fear of man is a snare, but the one who trusts in the Lord is protected. Lord, I know You are with me; You cover me. Father, who can be against me if You are for me? I declare I have the victory over fear because You have given me the victory in Jesus' name. I pray. Amen!

Scripture References

2 Timothy 1:7, 1 John 4:18, Isaiah 41:10, Jeremiah 1:8, Proverbs 29:25, Romans 8:31

A Prayer Against Pride

Lord, help me walk in humility all the days of my life. Show me where there is pride in my life and remove it from my heart. I know You resist the proud but give grace to the humble. Father, help me to do nothing in conceit but in humility, always considering others more important than myself. I understand arrogance leads to strife, but wisdom is gained by those who take advice. Help me always to be humble enough to listen. Lord, I realize pride comes before destruction and an arrogant spirit before a fall. Lord, help me to be clothed with humility, humble myself under Your Mighty hand, and allow You to exalt me. Father, help me never to think more highly of myself than I should. I understand the humble are blessed and will inherit the earth, so I willingly humble myself before You, Lord, and lay down any area of pride in my life. In Jesus' name, I pray, Amen!

Scripture References

James 4:6, Philippians 2:3, Proverbs 13:10, 1 Peter 5:6, Romans 12:3, Matthew 5:5

A Prayer For Your Heart

Father God, I understand the heart is more deceitful and incurable than anything else. So, Father, I ask You to search me and know my heart; test me and know my concerns. See if there is any offensive way in me; lead me in the everlasting way. Where sin is present in my heart, I ask You, Lord, to create a clean heart for me and renew a steadfast spirit within me. I know the pure at heart are blessed and will see God, so I pray my heart will always remain pure. Father, I pray my heart will never become stoney or hard, but help me always to follow Your statutes and carefully observe Your ordinances. God, do not let my heart turn to any evil thing or perform wicked acts with people who sin. Lord, keep my heart pure all the days of my life. Lord, help me to always be kind and compassionate to others, forgiving them as you have forgiven me. Help me to love my enemies and pray for those who persecute me. Lord, show me how to release toxic people in my life and give me the grace to pray for those who are challenging to deal with. Lord, heal me from all hurts and disappointments. I know You are near to the brokenhearted and save the crushed in spirit. Father, help me to always process my pain in an emotionally healthy way. Lord, help me to be an emotionally healthy person and operate that way in all my relationships. In Jesus' name, I pray, Amen!

Scripture References

Jeremiah 17:9, Psalm 139:23-24, Psalm 51:10, Matthew 5:8, Ezekiel 36:27, Psalm 141:4, Ephesians 4:32, Matthew 5:44, Psalm 34:18

99

A Prayer For Your Mouth

Father, I come to You today praying for my mouth. I ask You to help me speak words that would only bring healing and life to people. I do not want my tongue to speak devious words that break a person's spirit. Father, help me always respond gently because I know a gentle response turns away anger, but a harsh word stirs up wrath. Lord, I know the mouth of a fool blurts out foolishness, so keep me from foolish words. Lord, set up a guard for my mouth; keep watch at the door of my lips. I understand death and life are in the power of the tongue, and those who love it will eat its fruit. Father, let me eat the words of good fruit because of the good words flowing from my mouth. Help me to be discerning in my words. Father, show me when to speak and when to be silent. Father, let no foul language come from my mouth, but only what is good for building up individuals who need it. Let my words give grace to those who hear them. Father, help me rebuke those who need it in love because I know Your Word says it is better to experience open rebuke than hidden love. So, Father, help me address every situation in love. Help me speak words of love when correction is needed and when I speak up for myself against any injustices towards me. In Jesus' name, Amen!

Scripture References

Proverbs 15:4, Proverbs 15:1, Proverbs 15:2, Psalm 141:3,Proverbs 18:21, Ephesians 4:29, Proverbs 27:5

Prayer For Your Mind

Father, in the name of Jesus, I pray for my mind. Help me not to worry about anything, but in everything, through prayer and petition with thanksgiving, present my request to You, and the peace that surpasses all understanding will guard my heart and mind in Christ Jesus. Father, I pray I will only dwell on the things that are true, honorable, just, pure, lovely, and commendable, and anything that has moral excellence and is praiseworthy will be my thoughts. God, help me to take every thought captive to obey Christ. I thank You, Father, for allowing me to cast all my cares on You because You care about me. You told me not to worry about tomorrow because tomorrow will worry about itself, and each day has enough trouble of its own. So, I thank You, Lord, that I can trust You to handle every situation I am worried about. I declare I am being renewed in the spirit of my mind. I declare I have the mind of Christ. In Jesus' name, Amen!

Scripture References

Philippians 4:6-8, 2 Corinthians 10:5, 1 Peter 5:7, Matthew 6:34, Ephesians 4:23, 1 Corinthians 2:16

A Prayer For Wisdom

Father, I come to You today asking You for wisdom because I know wisdom is supreme. You said in Your Word that if I lack wisdom, I should ask for it, and You will generously and ungrudgingly give it to me. So, Father God, help me walk significantly in Your wisdom, not the wisdom of the earthly, unspiritual, and demonic world. Lord, allow me to never be wise in my own eyes but instead trust in You with all my heart and never rely on my understanding. Help me to know You in all my ways and know that You will make my paths straight. I realize that many plans are in a person's heart, but the Lord's decree will prevail. God, I know that I gain understanding from Your precepts. Lord, I recognize Your Word is a lamp for my feet and light on my path. Father, I believe the Lord establishes my steps and takes pleasure in my way. So I choose to rest, knowing that as I pray for Your guidance and will, You hear and always guide me in everything. In Jesus' name, I pray, Amen!

Scripture References

James 1:5, James 3:15, Proverbs 3:7, Proverbs 3:5-6, Proverbs 19:21, Psalm 119:104, Psalm 119:105, Psalm 37:23

A Prayer For Strength

Father, I come to You in the Mighty name of Jesus, the name that is above every name. I ask You to strengthen me. I know it is You who gives strength to the weary and strengthens the powerless. Help me to trust in You to give me the strength I am asking for. I know those who trust in the Lord will renew their strength; they will soar on wings like eagles; they will run and not become weary, they will walk and not faint. Lord, help me to resist the devil firmly in the faith, knowing the same kind of suffering is being experienced by my fellow believers throughout the world. Father, I know the God of all grace, who called me to His eternal glory in Christ, will restore, establish, strengthen, and support me after I have suffered a little while. I know I will experience suffering in this world, but I will be courageous because I know Jesus has conquered the world. Father, thank You for allowing me to be more than a conqueror through Jesus Christ. Father, help me endure hardship as a good soldier of Christ Jesus, always putting on the full armor of God so I can stand against the schemes of the devil. I realize my struggle is not against flesh and blood, but against the rulers, against the authorities, against the cosmic powers of this darkness, against evil, spiritual forces in the heavens, but I know I have the victory because of Jesus. I know all things work together for my good, and nothing can separate me from the love of God. Lord, I thank You for never leaving me or abandoning me. In Jesus' name, Amen!

Scripture References

Isaiah 40:29, Isaiah 40:31, 1 Peter 5:9, 1 Peter 5:10, John 16:33, Romans 8:37, 2 Timothy 2:3, Ephesians 6:11, Ephesians 6:12-13, 1 Corinthians 15:57, Romans 8:28, Romans 8:39, Hebrews 13:5

A Keeping Prayer For The Husband

Father, I pray for my husband. Lord, I pray that You would keep his mind and strengthen him to handle the pressures of life. Cover him and protect him from anything that would bring harm into his life—anything that would be detrimental to him physically, mentally, emotionally, and spiritually. Lord, help him always make wise choices in all areas of his life. I declare he understands the importance of making a covenant with his eyes, not to look and lust upon another woman. Help him remember the forbidden woman is bitter as wormwood and sharp as a double-edged sword. Help him always remember that her feet go down to death, her steps head straight for Sheol. Remind him she doesn't consider the path of life and she doesn't know her ways are unstable. Lord, help my husband to always keep his way from her. Father, I pray he would never go near the door of her house. Let him never give up his vitality or his years. May his finances, resources, and hard-earned money never become drained or end up in a foreigner's house. Let his physical body never be consumed. Let him never come to complete ruin because of sexual sins. I pray he would never lose himself to a forbidden woman. I pray my husband never operates like the wicked man who allows his iniquities to trap him. May he never become entangled in the ropes of his sin and die or become lost because of great stupidity. Father, help him discern what stupidity is. I pray he will always drink water from his own well. Father, never allow him to share his streams with another. I pray my husband will always take pleasure in me, the wife of his youth. Let my breasts always satisfy him. May he be lost in my love forever. Let him always find me captivating. Let him find no imperfections in me. May he be delighted with my entire appearance. Help me always capture his heart. I pray he always finds my caresses delightful. May the caresses of my hands and the scent of my body be better than wine to him. May the kisses of my mouth be sweet like honey to him. Father, help my words to always be pleasant and sweet like the honeycomb to my husband. I pray I will always be a wife of noble character to my husband who never causes shame for him. Father, help me to never just focus on my outward beauty but instead on what is inside of my heart, the imperishable quality of a gentle and quiet spirit. God, these things are of great worth in Your sight. I pray the heart of my husband can always trust in me. Father, help me to reward him with good all the days of my life. In Jesus' name, Amen!

Scripture References

Job 31:1, Proverbs 5:3-6, Proverbs 5:7-23, Proverbs 5:15-19, Song of Songs 4:1-11, Proverbs 16:24, Proverbs 12:4, 1 Peter 3:3-4, Proverbs 31:11-12

A Keeping Prayer For The Wife

Father God, I pray for my wife. Remind her she is made in Your image and after Your likeness. I pray she will not allow the enemy to whisper lies into her ear and will recognize when the enemy is causing her to walk in deception. Father, I pray she would realize when the enemy feeds her half-truths to discourage her. Help her always remember what God has said about her. Father, help her to remember how and why You created her. God, help her to remember she is my corresponding help, bone of my bone and flesh of my flesh, one with me. I pray she knows she is God's divine answer to my loneliness. Lord, remind her she is my good thing, and I have favor from You because of her. May her insecurities never cause her to question her worth to You or me. Help her to see her internal and external beauty. Remind her I always see it as well. Father, I pray her emotions never get the best of her. I pray she doesn't become a nagging and hot-tempered wife when she feels overwhelmed, disappointed, hurt, or frustrated. Remind her Your Word teaches it is better to live on the corner of a roof than to share a house with a nagging wife. Lord, help her to voice her concerns and frustrations in a respectful and emotionally healthy way. Lord, help me to be a safe space and give her the liberty to do so. Lord, help me to die to my pride and lay down any insecurity so I am receptive when my wife is concerned, disappointed, or hurt. Help me to love her like Christ loves the church. Teach me to care for her properly and show her unconditional, sacrificial love, always ensuring I am never bitter or unwise in my understanding of her. Help me to appreciate her and never take her for granted. Father, help me always to desire her only. Lord, help me continue dating, romancing, and complimenting her. Lord, I pray I will always desire intimacy with my wife and not just seek to fulfill my own sexual needs. Father, I pray that as I love her this way, she will always desire to submit to me in everything pleasing in the sight of God. In Jesus' name, Amen!

Scripture References

Genesis 2:27, Genesis 3:1-7, Genesis 2:20-24, Genesis 2:18, Proverbs 18:22, Song of Songs 1:5-6, Proverbs 31:30, Proverbs 21:19, Proverbs 25:24, Ephesians 5:25-29, Colossians 3:19, 1 Peter 3:7, Ephesians 5:24

A Prayer For Your Children

Father, I come to You in the Mighty name of Jesus, praying for my children and declaring that as for me and my house, we will serve the Lord. Father, help me to bring them up in the training and instruction of the Lord. Father, help me give them what they need and never become passive with my children's involvement. Help me always to hear them out and allow them to express their thoughts and feelings in a healthy, respectful way. Lord, help me to be a safe place for my children to come and share their hearts. I pray they never depart from Your way. I pray they will listen closely to wisdom and direct their hearts toward understanding. Help them realize the Lord gives wisdom, knowledge, and understanding from His mouth. Help them to see the blessing in always seeking the wisdom of God and never seeking the advice of the wicked or taking their path. I pray my children will never be yoked together with those who do not believe. I pray they have no partnership with lawlessness or fellowship with darkness. Father, I pray they find no rest, peace, comfort, or joy in sin. I pray they would know their delight is in the Lord's instruction and they meditate on it day and night. Help them to walk by the Spirit, so they will not carry out the desire of the flesh. Father, keep them from sexual immorality, moral impurity, promiscuity, idolatry, sorcery, hatred, strife, jealousy, outbursts of anger, selfish ambitions, dissensions, factions, envy, drunkenness, carousing, and anything similar. Help them to realize that those who belong to Christ Jesus have crucified the flesh with its passions and desires. May they always desire to cleanse themselves from every impurity of the flesh and spirit, bringing holiness to completion in the fear of God. Father, I pray that my children will not stir up or awaken love before the appropriate time. May they acknowledge that their season of singleness is a benefit to them and a time to be devoted to serving the Lord without distractions. Help them patiently and confidently wait on You for a godly spouse who will serve, honor, love, and worship You, Lord, with all their heart, soul, mind, and strength. I pray my children will always glorify You with their bodies. Help them to remember the body is not for sexual immorality but for the Lord. May they quickly flee from sexual immorality. I pray my daughters would never seek out attention by dressing provocatively like the thirsty woman. But let them always dress modestly, displaying class and virtue. May they always drink from the well of water springing up in them for eternal life—the living water of Jesus Christ. I pray my son will remember that marrying is better than burning with desire. But I pray he would not go into covenant with the wrong woman because he lacked self-control. Father, help my son to keep himself until marriage, knowing his body is the temple of the Holy Spirit. I pray all these things for my children in Jesus' name, Amen!

Scripture References

Ephesians 6:4, Proverbs 22:6, Proverbs 2:2, Proverbs 2:6, Psalm 1:1-2, 2 Corinthians 6:14, Galatians 5:16, Galatians 5:19-21, Galatians 5:24, 2 Corinthians 7:1, Song of Songs 8:4, 1 Corinthians 7:35, Mark 12:30, 1 Corinthians 6:20, 1 Corinthians 6:13, 1 Corinthians 6:18, 1 Timothy 2:9, John 4:14, 1 Corinthians 7:8, 1 Corinthians 6:19

A Prayer For Your Marriage

Father, I pray for my marriage. Lord, help us to communicate with one another effectively. Break down every communication barrier in our marriage. Let no foul language come from our mouths but only what is good for building one another up. Uproot every lie, accusation, and spirit of deception in our marriage that would keep us entangled in strife and confusion. Remove any spirit of rage, vindictiveness, defensiveness, and selfishness. Help us see each other through pure eyes and a pure heart. Father, help us hear one another and listen carefully to what we both are conveying. Help us to respect each other's opinions and differences as the opposite sex and as individuals. Heal us of those things that have hurt one another and caused us to operate in the spirit of bitterness. Where trust has been broken, Lord, I ask that You restore that trust into our marriage. Help us to see when the enemy is feeding us lies and using us to bring accusations against one another. Heal us from past traumatic relationships that have contaminated our perspective on relationships. I know you are a healer of the brokenhearted. Free us from perceptions of relationships and communication apart from You, Lord. Free us from unhealthy soul ties, childhood trauma, and every other traumatic experience that has affected us mentally and emotionally, causing us to operate with toxic behavior in our marriage.

Father, I realize to be made free by You is to be free indeed. Deliver us from pride, arrogance, vanity, sarcasm, fear, low self-esteem, and insecurities. Lord, help us to walk in total restoration because it is You who gives beauty for ashes. Help us to walk in humility, vulnerability, transparency, respect, and love. Help us to walk in total forgiveness. Help us to be compassionate to each other, continuously extending grace and mercy toward one another, remembering we both will make mistakes. Remind us, Father, we are both imperfect people. Lord, strip us of unrealistic expectations of one another. Help us always refer back to Your Word when facing a difficult matter. When the enemy comes in with confusion, remind us we can withstand him because a threefold cord is not quickly broken. Lord, help us to remember our house is built on the Solid Rock of Jesus Christ. Father, show us how to implement these requests into our lives daily. We know that only by Your Spirit can we do so. In Jesus' name, Amen!

Scripture References

Ephesians 4:29, John 8:44, Revelation 12:10, James 3:16, James 1:19-20, Ephesians 4:31, Psalm 147:3, John 8:36, Isaiah 61:3, Matthew 18:21-22, Ephesians 4:32, Galatians 5:15-16, Ecclesiastes 4:12, Matthew 7:24

A Prayer For Finances

Father, I pray for my finances. Help me to always honor You with them. As I honor you with my finances, I pray my barns will be completely filled and my vats will overflow with new wine. Help me to remember it is more blessed to give than receive. Father, Your Word says kindness to the poor is a loan to the Lord, and You will reward the lender. So, I thank You for rewarding me as I give generously to people experiencing financial difficulties. I pray I would never give to be seen by people, but it would always be done secretly and with a pure motive. Help me always to be a generous giver, continually reaping generosity. I pray I will give as I have decided in my heart, not reluctantly or out of compulsion because I know You love a cheerful giver. Father, may I always remember You provide seed for the sower and bread for food. I pray You would multiply my seed and increase the harvest of my righteousness. I pray You would supply all my needs according to Your riches and glory in Christ Jesus. Father, keep me from worrying about my life, what I will eat, drink, or my body, what I will wear. You said the Gentiles eagerly seek all these things, and You know I need them. So, Father, help me to seek You first and never worry about tomorrow but allow tomorrow to worry about itself because each day has enough trouble of its own. Father, as You increase me financially, I pray I never become a financial hoarder. I pray I will sow great seed as You increase me with great wealth. Father, use me to be a channel to fund Your kingdom and bless Your people. Father, I pray for generational wealth because Your Word says that a good man leaves an inheritance to his grandchildren. Father, I declare that I am a great steward of my finances, and like the ant, I carefully store up for the future. I declare as I remain diligent in what You have instructed me to do, it is leading me to profit. Father, open doors in my life that no man can close and prevent me from walking into doors or opportunities You did not create for me. Lord, help me seize every God opportunity that awaits me and not allow fear to keep me from receiving what You want to release into my hands. Lord, as I await Your promises for my life, help me to be content in all circumstances. Father, help me to appreciate what You have already blessed me with and not compare my situation or life with anyone else. In Jesus' name, I pray, Amen!

Scripture References

Proverbs 3:9-10, Acts 20:35, Proverbs 19:17, Matthew 6:3-4, 2 Corinthians 9:6-7, 2 Corinthians 9:10, Philippians 4:19, Matthew 6:25, Matthew 6:30, Matthew 6:31-34, Proverbs 13:22, Proverbs 6:6-11, Proverbs 21:5, Revelation 3:8, Philippians 4:12

A Prayer For Healing

Lord, I come before You today asking You for healing because You are the same God yesterday, today, and forever. The same God that healed the sick raised the dead, opened the eyes of the blind, caused the lame to walk, the deaf to hear, the mute to speak, and cast out demons. You are that same miracle-working God, and I believe Your power is still active today. So, Father, I humbly ask You to bring healing and restoration to my body. Your Word says healing is the children's bread, and I am Your child, so I ask You to heal me, Lord. I ask you to heal me from the crown of my head to the soles of my feet. Restore me, Jesus. Heal every imbalance in my body. Heal every tissue, muscle, cell, bone, and organ in my body. I know You can heal me, but even if I do not experience healing on this side of heaven, I will still give You glory because I know Your grace is sufficient for me. Father, I know You cause all things to work together for my good. Lord, as I pray for physical healing, I also ask for wisdom. Show me how to care for myself and help me to walk in discipline when the temptation to eat unhealthy foods arises. Lord, help me focus on the benefits of exercise and not the challenge or pain it causes to achieve my health goals. Father, I desire to experience the healing I am praying for. So, whatever it takes to receive my healing, I will do it. Lord, I pray this in Jesus' name, Amen!

Scripture References

Hebrews 13:8, Matthew 4:23, Matthew 9:18 & 22-25, Matthew 9:27-31, Matthew 4:24, Mark 1:23-26, Matthew 15:26, Mark 7:27, Daniel 3:18, 2 Corinthians 12:9, Romans 8:28, 1 Corinthians 9:27

A Prayer For The Church

Father, I come to You, praying for the church. I pray we will turn our hearts back to You. Father, help us to diligently and passionately pursue You, our first love. Help us to see how far we have fallen. I pray we will lay down our idols and worship You. Father, help us to keep ourselves from idols. Help us to seek You first, Your kingdom and righteousness. Father, I pray we would go into all the world and preach the gospel of Jesus Christ. I pray we will be Your witnesses throughout the earth. Father, show us how to care for those the carnal man considers less than by providing food and drink for those hungry and thirsty. I pray we will welcome the stranger, clothe the naked, and visit those sick and imprisoned. I pray we will always stand for righteousness. Father, help us to be bold as a lion. I pray we let our light shine so men see our good works and glorify You, Lord. Help us to be wise as serpents and innocent as doves. I pray we will always be prepared to make a defense to anyone who asks us for a reason for the hope that is in us. I pray we will always do it with gentleness and respect. Father, help us never be ashamed of the gospel because we recognize it is the power of God for salvation to everyone who believes. Father, I pray we will teach Your unadulterated Word and not add or take anything away from Your holy scripture. Father, I pray we won't just be hearers of Your Word deceiving ourselves but will always be doers of Your Word. Father, I pray we would rid ourselves of all moral filth and the evil that is so prevalent and humbly receive the implanted Word, which is able to save our souls. Father, help us to walk by the Spirit, so we will not carry out the desires of the flesh. Father, I pray we will not become conceited, provoking, or envious of one another. Lord, help us remember we are one body with many parts. Help us remember we need one another to do Your kingdom work; we are all valuable. Lord, help us to be all You designed us to be and never try to walk in someone else's purpose. Help us to care for one another, knowing if one person suffers, we all suffer with them, and if one is honored, we all rejoice with them. Father, show us how to love our neighbor as ourselves. Father, I thank You for making us emotionally and spiritually healthy and showing us how to love ourselves in a balanced way so we can love others. Father, I pray we will always make Your house a house of prayer. I pray we will worship You in Spirit and truth, all the days of our lives. In Jesus' name, Amen!

Scripture References

Revelation 2:4-5, 1 Corinthians 10:14, 1 John 5:21, Matthew 6:33, Mark 16:15, Acts 1:8, Matthew 25:35-40, Proverbs 28:1, Matthew 5:16, Matthew 10:16, 1 Peter 3:15, Romans 1:16, Revelation 22:18-19, James 1:22, James 1:21, Galatians 5:16, Galatians 5:26, 1 Corinthians 12:12-25, 1 Corinthians 12:26, Matthew 22:39, Matthew 21:13, John 4:24

A Prayer of Salvation For Loved Ones

Father, I come to you in the Mighty name of Jesus, praying for the salvation of my family and friends. Lord, I pray they would call on Your name because Your Word declares those who call on the name of the Lord shall be saved. Father, I pray they would confess with their mouth and believe in their hearts that God raised Jesus from the dead, resulting in their salvation. Your Word also says today is the day of salvation, so I pray those who did not receive Your salvation yesterday receive it today. Father, remove a heart of stone and put in a heart of flesh. Lord, give them a desire to know You. Help them to realize You are the Way, the Truth, and the Life and no one comes to the Father except through You. Father, help them draw near to You so You can draw near to them. Lord, let them find no rest, peace, joy, or comfort in sin. Father, allow them to become highly convicted and uncomfortable by their sinful lifestyle. Lord, give them dreams and visions of heaven and hell. Father, help them realize they are broken, lost, and in need of the saving grace of Jesus. Help them to recognize the enemy wants to destroy them, and the only way they can have true victory over the enemy is through the Spirit of the living God. Father, I pray they will desire a personal, intimate relationship with You. Show them the difference between religious practices and a relationship with You. Break the spirit of deception off of their lives. Father, I pray they will not harden their hearts in rebellion as they hear Your voice calling them out of darkness. Lord, I pray for the one who has backslid. I pray they will turn their hearts back to you. Help them see You never left them, even in their mess. I pray they would realize You are waiting for them to repent and return. I pray they will run back into the loving arms of Jesus. I pray as You knock at the door of their hearts, they will allow You to come in. I pray all these things in the matchless and powerful name of Jesus! Amen!

Scripture References

Romans 10:13, Romans 10:9, 2 Corinthians 6:2, Ezekiel 36:26, John 14:6, James 4:8, Hebrews 3:15, Jeremiah 3:14-15, Revelation 3:20

A Prayer To Ask God Into Your Heart

If you do not know or have a relationship with the Lord, I encourage you to pray about getting to know Him. Giving my life to the Lord was the best decision of my life. It is as easy as 1, 2, 3. All you have to do is acknowledge you are a sinner and need the saving grace of Jesus Christ. You don't have to do anything to earn salvation because Jesus freely gave it to you, but you will have to partner with the Holy Spirit to experience the change and freedom God wants you to have from sin. Just say this prayer, and it is as simple as that.

Salvation Prayer

Lord, I come to You, acknowledging I am a sinner and need the saving grace of Jesus. I confess Jesus is Lord. I confess He died on the cross and rose from the dead for my sins. I repent of my sins and ask You to come into my heart and change my life, Jesus. Lord, help me walk in righteousness. Wash me, Lord, change my heart, make me new in You. I desire to have an intimate personal relationship with you, Lord. I want to live for YOU forever. In Jesus' name, Amen!

I want to encourage you with this. Some people make Christianity seem as if you will get what you want all the time. Not true. We will not always get what we want when we want it. It will be hard at times to do the right thing. For instance, when someone has wronged you for no apparent reason, you may be tempted to try to avenge yourself, but the Holy Spirit may prompt you to let the offense go. Life will be challenging sometimes, and you may want to give up on God, but please don't. We are going to experience suffering as believers. In your suffering, remember the end result is greater than that trial. Remember, heaven is our ultimate goal, and one day, our pain and suffering will no longer exist (Revelation 21:4).

Also, surround yourself with a great community of believers, those who will help you live a Christian lifestyle. Get involved in a Connect group. Get actively involved in serving in your church in some capacity. Many people fall away when they don't get connected. They may feel lonely and overlooked, especially if the congregation is big. Falling away is an opportunity for the enemy to pull you back into the same habits, so get connected and stay connected. Your life depends on it.

Lastly, spend your personal time with the Lord. Read your Bible daily, pray daily, attend Bible studies, attend church events and outreaches, and focus on learning and growing in God. As you pursue God, you will see changes in your heart and life.

Welcome to the family, my friend!

Scripture References
    Acts 16:31, Romans 10:9, John 3:16

End

137

Don't miss out!

Visit the website below and you can sign up to receive emails whenever Q. ELI publishes a new book. There's no charge and no obligation.

https://books2read.com/r/B-A-SSFEB-GEUAC

About the Author

Q Eli, is a native of Louisiana. She is a Christian woman who has been married to her husband for 20 plus years. She is a mother of 3 children. Q, is a teacher of the gospel, marriage coach, health coach, entrepreneur, and content creator.

Read more at https://justqeli.com/.